SCHOLASTIC

YOU CAN

Use an interactive WHITE BOARD

Consultant Editor:
Julie Cogill

FOR AGES
4-7

"There is a whiteboard revolution in UK schools"
Primary National Strategy

D1312883

Consultant Editor
Julie Cogill

Illustrations
Mike Phillips

Authors
Julie Cogill
Karen Mawer
Heather Cromie
Anne Cooper

Series Designer
Catherine Mason

Designer
Melissa Leeke

Additional Authors
Jon Audain
Anthony David
Sara Fielder
Martin Flute

Editor
Frances Ridley

Assistant Editor
Niamh O'Carroll

Cover concept/designer
Anna Oliwa

Cover illustration
© stockbyte/punchstock;
SMART Board Interactive Whiteboard © SMART Technologies Inc

Text © 2006 Julie Cogill, Karen Mawer
Heather Cromie, Anne Cooper

© 2006 Scholastic Ltd

Designed using Adobe InDesign

Published by Scholastic Ltd
Villiers House
Clarendon Avenue
Leamington Spa
Warwickshire CV32 5PR

www.scholastic.co.uk

Printed by Bell and Bain Ltd.
 3 4 5 6 7 8 9   6 7 8 9 0 1 2 3 4

Post-it is a registered trademark of 3M

British Library Cataloguing-in-Publication Data
A catalogue record for this book is available from the British Library.
ISBN 0-439-96539-X
ISBN 978-0439-96539-2

The rights of the authors have been asserted in accordance with the Copyright, Designs and
Patents Act 1988.

Contents

Contents

Introduction

What is an interactive whiteboard?

'Every class should have one!'

This comment about interactive whiteboards has been made by many teachers who have used them across the primary age groups. Many teachers believe that the interactive whiteboard is an important modern development that will bring about change in teaching and learning in the primary school.

The interactive whiteboard is attached to a computer so that images can be clearly projected on to the screen or whiteboard. It is different from using a projector because the board itself is sensitive to touch and operates as an interactive device. When the board is activated, and then touched with a finger or a special pen, it responds in exactly the same way as a computer screen responds to the manipulation of a mouse.

About this book

The 50 ideas presented in this book are about teaching and learning with an interactive whiteboard, and about how you can use ICT to create inspiring lessons. One question that often arises is whether using an interactive whiteboard is about teaching, learning or using ICT. The answer is that it's about all three. The interactive whiteboard will not do the teaching for you but it will give you access to many more resources – audio, video, images, websites and interactive activities – that were previously unavailable for the whole class to view, discuss, interact with and learn from.

The following comments were made by teachers who had used interactive whiteboards for one year:

'The boards stimulate the children's learning through the use of interactivity. We can access such a wide range of resources which would otherwise take us a long time to collect and we can share any work we do which is also a great time saver.'

(Key Stage 1 team leader)

'Children really enjoy seeing the big bright screen and they can see both text and images clearly. The board is invaluable when we are reading together and I can point things out in the pictures and label them on the screen'

(Year 1 teacher)

'I can share some of the teaching and learning with the children themselves. They can come to the front of the class and show the rest of the children their own ideas which they love doing.'

(Year 2 teacher)

'For young children it presents such a tactile resource. They can move objects around on the screen or watch me moving things and see what's happening so clearly. If we just use the mouse and a big screen then it feels much further away from what we are trying to do.'

(Reception teacher)

Whiteboards and teaching

At a basic level, the interactive whiteboard can be used as a chalkboard. Although this is not necessarily the best use of the available technology, the whiteboard does have many advantages over a traditional chalkboard in that multiple pages can be created. Work displayed at the beginning of a lesson can therefore be accessed at any time, with just the click of a button, if teachers want to review earlier teaching points. All the pages can be displayed or reviewed in sequence for ease of navigation. Other useful features include the ability to change colour instantly, and the availability of simple templates for tables or grids to help in organising points made in whole-class work. Using the whiteboard in this way will help new users to develop confidence and we hope that this book will also be a useful tool to get you started on your adventure into new ways of teaching and learning.

Whiteboards and learning

If you already have some experience in using the whiteboard, however, then we hope the teaching suggestions will take you further. What is especially important is the facility the whiteboard provides to share children's learning experiences. This does not mean just asking individual children to come to the board to suggest answers, but using the facilities of the board to display and discuss ideas so that everyone can share in the learning experience. The whiteboard also allows teachers to explore and relate the thinking of individuals to the context of the learning that is happening in the class as a whole. In the best whiteboard classrooms, teachers comment that sometimes they can stand aside while children themselves 'lead' the lesson by presenting their ideas to the class for further discussion.

Whiteboards and ICT

This book is not intended to teach ICT skills but it does provide ideas for how ICT can be used to create classroom resources for the whiteboard. There are particular hints on how you can use Microsoft Word, PowerPoint, Excel and resources found on the Internet to make lessons more interesting.

We hope you will add to the ideas presented in this book by using the photocopiable templates provided at the back of the book to record your own uses of the whiteboard. Last but not least, it is important to share both your whiteboard skills and ideas for teaching and learning with colleagues. Sharing skills and resources in this way will not only save you a great deal of time, but will also help to create a collaborative teaching community and enhance the learning experiences of children.

You Can... Use an interactive whiteboard to prepare lessons

One of the advantages of using a whiteboard is that lesson plans and content can be prepared away from the classroom in advance. Slides and flipchart pages can be prepared in advance. A whiteboard provides you with the opportunity to give high quality presentations, and to use a wide range of resources. Lessons can be planned and content loaded onto the board at appropriate times during the day, thereby leaving more time for teaching and learning!

Thinking points

● The design of your presentation should not take precedence over its content.

● Make sure the resources you use provide appropriate content and presentation for the age group you are teaching

● Think about the questions you use as you prepare flipcharts or slide shows. Use open, rather than closed, questions that draw on children's knowledge.

● Consider how children can engage in an interactive way. Is there potential for children to demonstrate what they can do at the board? Does the activity lend itself to a collaborative task, such as whole-class creative writing? (A photocopiable sheet has been provided on page 61 to help plan your whiteboard tasks.)

● Consider planning a programme of learning in advance, for example across three lessons, so that continuity and progression can be built in.

Tips, ideas and activities

● Be flexible! Pre-prepared slides or flipchart pages are useful but be prepared to take the lead from what children are learning and how the lesson develops. You don't have to stick to your 'script'.

● Keep an organised electronic file of all lessons, so that you can recall and adapt a lesson for a different learning experience. A file of hard-copy lessons is also useful for quick access. If children need to recap their existing knowledge, use the files to check how the topic was originally taught, and review appropriate pages before moving to new work.

● Build up a range of illustrations, demonstrations and visual aids (subject to copyright) to help retain children's attention and motivation and develop their understanding.

● When you are searching for resources, make a note of images, websites or video resources, copyright permitting, that may be useful for particular subjects, even if the resource is not immediately relevant. Many a frustrating hour can be spent looking for that 'perfect' image you saw early last week!

● Remember that children need to engage in their own learning and work independently for part of the lesson. Three slides and an illustration, together with questions, answers and discussion, can take a substantial slice of lesson time.

You Can... **Use an interactive whiteboard to show websites**

The use of websites can add much to a lesson, be it looking at images or viewing other children's work on the Internet. The interactive whiteboard is an obvious and excellent tool for displaying and navigating through the wealth of resources that can be found on the World Wide Web (www). There are literally millions of websites to choose from. Using a search engine, which is basically an index to a large number of websites, will help you to find what you want.

Thinking points

● If a website meets the needs of your objective then use it – it does not pay to spend hours looking for that perfect site!

● Using educational search engines such as the National Grid for Learning (www.ngfl.gov.uk) will reduce the amount of time you spend searching for appropriate content.

● Visit the site to check its suitability before using it with the whole class. Ask yourself:

1) Is the language accessible?

2) Is the font large enough?

3) Does the content of the site support your lesson objectives?

4) Can the children clearly see the text or images on the whiteboard? Do you need to modify the background?

● A firewall filters for keywords on a site and prevents the user from entering inappropriate sites by mistake. If your school has a firewall it is possible that a website you can access at home may not be available in school.

Tips, ideas and activities

● Use websites on the whiteboard to give children global experiences, for sources of evidence in history and to find out about the background of an author or literary text.

● Text and pictures can be copied from many websites, copyright permitting, by highlighting them (clicking and dragging the cursor over the desired area), copying them (Ctrl + C) and then pasting them (Ctrl + V) into a word processing document or on to an interactive whiteboard flipchart.

● Use the Favourites button, found on the Internet Task Bar, to store your favourite websites. By doing this, you will be able to return to websites more easily, particularly if you are in a hurry!

● As you load a website, explain to children the processes that you are using and which buttons you are clicking on with your pen or finger. This has obvious benefits for the children's ICT skills and you will quickly find that the children start to point out any errors that you make.

● If children have computer access ask them to continue their Internet use at home. (NB Make sure that you have checked and approved a website before recommending it to the children.)

You Can... **Use an interactive whiteboard to show video resources**

Video material offers a range of unique experiences that can transport children to worlds they might never otherwise experience. An interactive whiteboard enables video resources to be accessed efficiently. It allows you to integrate video much more easily within a lesson, without the need to move children or television monitors. The way you access film resources will depend on what equipment is available to you. Film resources may be accessed via a video recorder, a DVD, a CD-ROM, or downloaded from the web or a local server, copyright permitting. Without a very fast Internet connection, however, video streaming in a classroom is not advisable.

Thinking points

● Consider how the video links to the lesson and whether it will be used to introduce a topic, as a major resource in teaching a topic or to consolidate previous work.

● Think carefully about how much video to show. Since it is easy to access through the whiteboard, two or three minutes may be enough to illustrate a teaching point. On the other hand, 15 minutes may be required to give sufficient context to capture children's engagement and interest and to provide real learning.

● Preview the resource to consider where the video might be paused, so that children can predict what might happen next or to find out what children have previously understood. Pausing the video helps to give a more interactive experience.

Tips, ideas and activities

● You can use video to:
  ● show the wider world, through films of natural phenomena, animals in habitat, volcanoes, distant and inaccessible places and points of view from different people
  ● show the historical world, through archive film, examples of oral history and the dramatisation of historical events
  ● show the scientific world, through slow motion or time lapse images and the use of magnified images through an electron microscope
  ● show the emotional or inner world, through the experiences of different people, using case studies or drama reconstructions to encourage empathy with someone else's situation
  ● show the world of literature, through dramatisations
  ● move from the concrete to the abstract in mathematics, through a split screen or through images that gradually transform
  ● create motivation in what is to be learnt by the use of interesting case studies, animation, cartoons, humour and drama.

● After viewing, discuss with the children what the film sequence was about to help consolidate their learning

● Most importantly, if the video sequence uses humour or lends itself to joining in, encourage children to do this and enjoy it with them as a whole-class activity.

You Can... Use an interactive whiteboard for children's presentations

Many children enjoy showing and demonstrating their work in front of the class. Using the whiteboard, children's work can be displayed on a large screen so everyone can share and discuss it. Using programs such as Microsoft PowerPoint helps children to structure their work and produce professional presentations regardless of their level of attainment. Less confident learners in particular can succeed when using the computer – particularly those who struggle with written work. The computer will assist children in improving the presentation of their work which will help their self-esteem.

Thinking points

● Consider how much help the children will need with the main functions of the presentation software. For example, will they be able to plan the types of slide they will need to use? Do they know how to change fonts and type sizes? Can they add pictures?

● Consider asking pairs of children to share a presentation. The whiteboard can be a great vehicle for promoting collaborative learning.

● Consider which activities may be appropriate for children's presentations, for example:

● a presentation to the whole class by a small group demonstrating the work they have done

● a presentation by the class at assembly, to the whole school

● an account of a school visit by the class, for a parents evening.

● Think of different ways in which children can share their work with parents and other carers.

Tips, ideas and activities

● If children working in small groups are asked to provide a class presentation on an issue, encourage them to choose one in which they will want to participate, for example family pets.

● Discuss with children the conventions of writing for presentations, for example the need for clear and succinct text on each slide.

● Encourage the children to plan how they might find images for their presentations, for example Clip Art, the Internet (copyright permitting) or digital photographs.

● Encourage children to look for pictures that enhance the information in their presentations, and that are not just decorative.

● Explain that slides will help the children to make their presentation look professional, but that the clarity and content of each slide is more important than its design.

● When presenting, many children might be tempted to just read out the contents of each slide. To begin with, allow them to do this to gain confidence. In time, encourage them to add more detail to their presentations, using the slides as prompts rather than scripts.

● Give children the opportunity to practise their presentations, so that they are clear and confident about what they are going to say.

● After the big event, congratulate the children and celebrate their success.

You Can... Use an interactive whiteboard for PowerPoint presentations

One of the greatest strengths of using a whiteboard is that information can be presented clearly. Words and pictures can be combined in a variety of interesting and colourful ways. Microsoft PowerPoint is a high-powered software tool designed to present text, charts, graphs, sound effects, video and animations in a dynamic slide show format. It is ideal for use on the interactive whiteboard. You can enhance you PowerPoint presentation by asking open-ended questions to develop discussion work and draw a more personal response from the children.

Thinking points

● Think carefully about the pace of your presentation. Avoid using too many slides. Break up the presentation by adding in 'Points to discuss', or a small activity.

● When presented with a range of information, how many of us read the smaller print? Don't put too much text on each slide and make sure the font size is large enough.

● Remember, 'A picture tells a thousand words': using pictures in your PowerPoint presentations can save time, money and resources. When pictures are enlarged on a whiteboard the whole class can share the resource easily.

● Think about the design and impact of each slide. The human eye is drawn to information that is large, clearly presented and uncluttered. Effective adverts use pictures and large text to convey a message. The same theory can be applied to presentations relating to teaching and learning. Large, clearly presented text and relevant, eye-catching pictures will be easier to understand.

Tips, ideas and activities

● Experiment by changing the background to your slides. A simple splash of colour or a pattern will liven up the screen. A cream background, rather than white, may be easier on the reader's eyes.

● Use effects sparingly. A presentation in which every sentence and picture is animated can be overbearing and leave the audience feeling pale and nauseous.

● Explore the use of the different Action Buttons. These buttons perform an action when pressed and offer a quick and easy way of linking pages together (this is known as hyperlinking). Below are examples of the different types of Action Buttons that can be inserted into a presentation:

● To insert an Action Button using PowerPoint:

1) Click on the Slide Show menu and then scroll down to Action Buttons.

2) A menu will appear displaying the different buttons that can be inserted into a presentation. By hovering the cursor over each button a label will appear, informing you of its function.

3) Click on the button required and a cross will appear.

4) Hold down the left-hand mouse button and drag the cross. Click where you want to position it and the Action Button will appear.

You Can... **Use an interactive whiteboard for effective starters**

The whiteboard offers a huge range of experiences to motivate visual, kinaesthetic and aural learning. Starter materials range from a few minutes of video and television footage, to websites, images from the software library or a blank board with the facility to write, draw, erase and save. An effective starter will highlight the context of what children will be learning by reflecting on previous learning. The whiteboard can help you to do this: for example, you could show a slide used in a previous lesson, but highlight new facts.

Thinking points

● Think about when the starter takes place. If children are coming into the classroom just before the lesson, display something that will grab their attention as they are settling down to work: a poem for the whole class to share, for example, or a simple number puzzle (*Which of these numbers are odd?* or *Which of these numbers are add to ten?*).

● Consider the timing of the starter. Avoid using complex resources or lengthy explanation.

● Vary the types of resources you use. If an image is over-used, its impact can be lost. Also, different resources will appeal and motivate different children.

● Consider the purpose of the starter and how the whiteboard might be used to highlight it. For example, the purpose might be to sharpen and rehearse skills, to identify facts which children should know or to review work done at home.

Tips, ideas and activities

● Use thought bubbles to record children's knowledge. If appropriate, ask children to suggest categories into which their ideas can be sorted, so the information is more accessible. Ask children to drag and drop their ideas into their chosen categories.

● Save children's initial ideas and return to them in the plenary session. Make a note of any new knowledge taught or learned during the lesson.

● Show children a series of images, for example a set of buildings, and ask them to explain what they have in common and what is different.

● Use a set of images to stimulate creative writing. Ask children to come to the board, sequence the images and then describe their stories. In this way several different stories may emerge, depending on how the images are sequenced.

● Suggest a new topic to children and ask them how they could find facts about this topic at the start of the lesson. Demonstrate the use of an Internet search engine such as www.google.co.uk to find links to new information.

● Start with a ten-minute video, television show or DVD. Use this to prompt speaking and listening activities such as debate, discussion and role play.

You Can... **Use an interactive whiteboard for effective plenary sessions**

The plenary session allows the teacher and children to summarise and reflect upon the learning, and highlight and tackle any misconceptions. A whiteboard makes it easy to revisit the main teaching objective. Images and information can be quickly referred to, in the order in which they were taught, from any saved flipchart pages. If misconceptions have arisen, flipchart pages can be annotated with another colour and resaved for follow-up lessons. The activity could be remodelled with different images and used again to reinforce the learning, perhaps in a subsequent starter.

Thinking points

● Consider the timing of the plenary session. The lesson may be just before a break, when children are tired or have lost concentration. Children should be asked to remain focused for no more than ten minutes.

● Concentration often wanes during plenary sessions. Consider using different media, such as websites, games, television or video clips to reinforce concepts and refocus the children.

● Think about using different visual images from those used in the main part of the lesson to emphasise the learning objective, but explain them in the same way.

● Think about how you might refer back to saved flipchart pages to analyse the lesson and aid future planning

● Consider the different purposes of a plenary session and how the whiteboard might be used to highlight these. For example, ask children to present or explain their work, draw together key learning points, or make links to other work.

Tips, ideas and activities

● When children are feeding back, encourage them to illustrate what they have learned using the Pen function on a blank flipchart page. Children's writing is often small, so enlarge it for the whole class to see.

● If time is available, scan in some of the children's work, so that they can present and explain it to the whole class.

● Depending on what equipment is available, children can be filmed during the main part of the lesson, especially for a role play, drama or PE lesson. Always obtain permission from parents before filming or photographing children. Use the video to recap and evaluate lesson activities during the plenary session.

● Compare and contrast a short video clip with that taught in the main part of the lesson. For example, if the main part of the lesson considered historical artefacts, use a clip showing those artefacts in use.

● Visit a website that is related to the lesson. For example, if the children have been looking at a painting, visit an art gallery website to show how a range of different artists have painted similar subjects.

● Ask the children to tell you what they have learnt during the lesson and write this down for everyone to see. You can then save the contents of the board for your assessment records.

You Can... **Use an interactive whiteboard to revise and consolidate earlier work**

Any document or flipchart you have created can be saved on to the computer to create a bank of saved lessons that can be accessed at any time to revise a selected objective. This is particularly effective when revisiting learning objectives from earlier in a week and clarifying any misconceptions. If you are conducting more formal revision sessions, for example before moving onto related work in the same topic, the BBC website (www.bbc.co.uk/ schools) offers plenty of models, guides and lesson ideas to help you and your class, both at home and in school.

Thinking points

● What is the purpose of the revision? Remember to keep the lesson succinct and to the point. It is important that the children review only past objectives, and that skills are consolidated as well as content. Ensure that new objectives do not creep in inadvertently.

● The whiteboard can help you to keep revision fresh. Consider different ways of presenting the topic, for example through video clips, websites and animations.

● Consider ways to involve the children with the revision session. The interactive whiteboard appeals to kinaesthetic and visual learners: involve these children in leading the session by showing previous work or demonstrating skills.

● Revisit previously-saved lesson ideas – particularly any children's work. Saved material will trigger past learning experiences and can be used to address any misconceptions.

Tips, ideas and activities

● Use multiple-choice tests on the whiteboard. These can be easily prepared in PowerPoint using text and Action Buttons (see page 11). Check that all children can see the multiple choice options clearly, as the dropdown menus sometimes have very small text. Ask the whole class to look at the options for each question and to vote for the correct one. Alternatively, ask why the other options are incorrect. Questions are often cleverly constructed to draw out common misconceptions.

● Visit your whiteboard supplier's website. Such websites often offer a rich source of pre-prepared lessons that can be downloaded and used for consolidation.

● Visit the National Literacy and Numeracy sites. Many of the resources can be accessed and edited on screen, in the same way that you would edit any screen shot. This allows you to prepare enlarged, clean copies of the resources rather than relying on smaller, A3, black-and-white photocopies.

How many apples?

a. 5 ☐

b. 9 ☐

c. 7 ☐

You Can... Use an interactive whiteboard to share effective teaching

The arrival of an interactive whiteboard often generates excitement, enthusiasm and anticipation amongst teaching staff. Actually using the whiteboard, however, can be a roller-coaster experience. There are the highs when things go right and the full potential of the whiteboard is realised; and there are the lows when the technology fails to do what is wanted. It is important to share different experiences, in order to share effective practice and further teaching and learning.

Thinking points

● Think about who is available for help when whiteboard problems occur: for example, the ICT co-ordinator, another colleague or the most ICT-competent children in your class.

● Make sure that lines of communication with technical support are established and kept open.

● Changing ways of teaching is an exciting challenge and there are plenty of opportunities for change when using a whiteboard. Be optimistic when developing your skills, and experiment – after all, there's always the manual for back-up!

● Consider what the word 'effective' means in terms of teaching. (The dictionary defines it as 'producing the desired effect'.) The most effective whiteboard activities are interactive. When planning, consider what the children could do at the whiteboard during the lesson. If you 'deliver' the lesson without involving them, the potential interactivity will be lost.

Tips, ideas and activities

● Don't use the whiteboard for every lesson. Produce materials targeted at one subject area, that will actively engage the children.

● Consider 'team-teaching' to begin with. Try to:
  ● plan lessons with a colleague in the same year group if possible and share the preparation load
  ● arrange your planning meetings in the same room as the whiteboard, activities can then be tried out and discussed
  ● follow up your jointly planned lesson by considering how effective the lesson was for each class of children, and modifying appropriately
  ● keep a shared electronic file of lessons plans for the year group.

● When interactivity is encouraged, collaborative learning with lots of discussion between the children flourishes. Make sure all your children are actively participating in the lesson.

● Scanned images can be used in presentations subject to copyright. Share images with colleagues and build up a library of suitable images for the whole school to draw upon.

● Share your experiences, for example:
  ● set up an 'Ideas' section on the school network
  ● invest in memory sticks so all ideas can be shared
  ● set aside some staff meeting time to discuss successes and disappointments, and to share information and advice.

You Can... **Use an interactive whiteboard to teach ICT**

There are many ICT applications in the classroom, and learning how to use ICT can be a daunting task. The interactive whiteboard can be used to enhance children's learning about ICT. The computer screen and its contents can be projected onto the whiteboard, enabling the whole class to benefit from the demonstration of software and hardware and their applications. Also, photos of ICT applications being used in 'real-life' situations can help to set a context for children's learning.

Thinking points

● Consider ways in which the whiteboard could be used to model ICT skills. Any application that runs on a computer can be displayed on a whiteboard, making it an ideal tool to introduce new skills in any application: use of the mouse, how to point and click, word processors, using CDs and the Internet, and so on. Use the whiteboard to demonstrate specific skills and to explain how children might work independently.

● Think about how the whiteboard may be used to demonstrate just how the mouse works. Younger children may find it difficult to understand the link between the mouse and the computer, and the whiteboard can help to bridge this gap since it gives a much more tactile experience.

● The language of computers is often a barrier to progress. When performing procedural tasks, such as booting up the computer, clicking an icon or moving the cursor, talk the children through the process so they become familiar with technical terms.

Tips, ideas and activities

● As children develop confidence with computers and the complexity of their tasks increases, it becomes ever more important that they manage files and navigate the machine effectively. Use the whiteboard to model opening and saving files (with sensible names), and starting and closing programs. The teacher is a role model for children and should aim to develop pupils' proficiency with the machine as well as individual programs.

● It's frustrating when children panic because they've pressed the wrong button or seemingly lost work. Show children common mistakes and how to correct them, for example, using the back button to undo the last action.

● Demonstrate the best position to type, using both hands. Explain the layout and purpose of letter, number and function keys. Encourage children to memorise the arrangement of keys to increase their typing speed by playing Blind Man's Buff.

● When teaching how to use particular software, if you have a whiteboard in the ICT suite, ask children to model what you are doing step by step until they become familiar with how the program works. It is then much easier to help them if they become confused and to set them back on the right track.

You Can... **Use an interactive whiteboard**
to teach shape

The whiteboard provides a wonderful opportunity to illustrate standard shapes in a colourful and interesting way. This is invaluable for lessons about shapes, but shapes are useful to illustrate other mathematical concepts, too. Shapes can easily be created and then displayed and presented ready for whole-class interaction. Creating a template with a range of standard shapes not only offers a tool for excellent and accurate presentations, but also enables the shapes to be saved for later use.

Thinking points

● Explore the different shapes that are available to you. All the common shapes are available either from the whiteboard's own software or through the use of the shape templates in Microsoft Word (see below).

● Consider different ways in which you can use shapes to illustrate other mathematical concepts. For example, shapes can be used for:

● encouraging children to describe repeating patterns

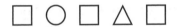

● for example, 'there are three types of shape in this pattern', 'every other shape is a square' and so on.

● illustrating simple fractions

● illustrating block graphs or pictograms.

Tips, ideas and activities

● To draw the common shapes using Word:
1) Click on View at the top of the screen and then click Toolbars. Tick the Drawing box. The Drawing Toolbar will appear at the bottom of the screen.

2) Click AutoShapes and point to the Basic Shapes category. Click on the shape you want.

● To insert a shape with a predefined size, click the document in which you want to display it.

● To insert a different-sized shape, drag the shape (using the surrounding handles) to the size you want. To keep the same ratio of shape, hold down Shift while you drag.

● To add colour, change borders, rotate the shape or add three-dimensional effects to it, select the object and then use the buttons on the Drawing Toolbar.

● A range of coloured shapes can be created on one page by repeating this process.

● Join two shapes together to produce more complex or more interesting shapes. For example, to create a basic house shape, drag and join a rectangle and a trapezium together. Draw the outline of each shape in the same colour and use the same colour-fill for each so that no black lines will show.

You Can... **Use an interactive whiteboard for oral/mental starters**

Using the whiteboard for oral and mental starters encourages the children to be fully involved in the lesson and caters in particular for the needs of the kinaesthetic learner. A range of Interactive teaching programs (ITPs) have been provided by the National Numeracy Strategy, free of charge. These allow you to begin using the interactive whiteboard in your oral and mental starters, with very little preparation of resources. The ideas below are by no means exhaustive, as the programs are very versatile.

Thinking points

● Think about the range of numbers that less able and more able children in your class work with for each activity. Consider whether the software program caters for this range or whether it will be necessary to offer extra support or an extension activity for some children.

● Consider how you might use the whiteboard pens to highlight or annotate key learning points while running the Interactive teaching program.

● Consider whether paper or apparatus-based methods will better suit the needs of the children. Although the whiteboard is a great resource, don't automatically assume that it is the best way to teach every oral and mental starter.

● Each of the activities described right refers to an Interactive teaching program. These can be accessed from www.standards.dfes .gov.uk/primary/publications/ mathematics/itps/

● Remember to save pages for assessment purposes, or to review and annotate in subsequent lessons.

Tips, ideas and activities

● 'Twenty cards' – Deal out some random number cards into rows. Turn over the cards and ask children to drag and drop them to order the numbers. Make a stack of cards with a set step number. Deal the cards and ask children to predict the next number in the sequence.

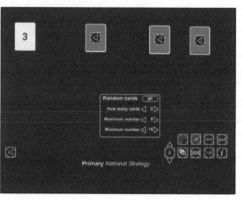

Twenty Cards – DfES Interactive teaching program

● 'Number grid' – Display a 100 square. Highlight the first few numbers in a number sequence and look at the pattern this creates. Ask children to continue the sequence. Mask out some numbers and let children work out what numbers are missing. Demonstrate how to calculate additions and subtractions using a 100 square.

● 'Number spinners' –Create three six-sided spinners and spin them to generate three numbers. Talk about the different strategies for adding three small numbers together and challenge the children to work out the answer.

● 'Difference' – Demonstrate the strategy for finding the difference between two numbers. Ask the children to work out the difference between two numbers and then check their answers by watching the program's animation.

● Copy and print the display screen by pressing the 'print screen' button and pasting the image into a program such as Microsoft Paint. Alternatively, use the Camera tool on your whiteboard software.

You Can... **Use an interactive whiteboard to show the results of class surveys**

Data handling in Key Stage 1 focuses more heavily on interpreting data than communicating it. Using the interactive whiteboard enables you to quickly compile the results of class surveys, and convert them into charts. This in turn allows the class to spend more time focusing on the interpretation of data and to spend much less time on drawing bar charts and pictograms. The whiteboard also allows every child in the class to see the data displayed clearly.

Thinking points

● Be aware of sensitivities that children might have when choosing a survey to carry out. For example, a survey of children's weight might cause distress for an overweight child.

● It is easier to collect and display discrete rather than continuous data at Key Stage 1. Continuous data, such as height, cannot be shown on a bar chart or pictogram unless a range of heights are bundled together.

● Consider the best way to display the results of the survey you are carrying out. Decide whether a table, pictogram or bar chart would be easiest to interpret.

● If you choose to use a bar chart to display the results, you will need to consider the scale that you will use on the vertical axis. Consider whether less able children will need support reading the scale.

Tips, ideas and activities

● Create a table of data for a bar chart in Microsoft Excel. Include appropriate headings and add borders. Do this by highlighting the relevant cells, selecting Format and then Cells. Press the Borders tab in the Format Cells box and select the style and colour of the border you want.

● Select the Chart Wizard icon on the standard Toolbar to insert a chart of the data. Use the Wizard to alter options for how the chart is displayed. Place the finished chart as an object in the original worksheet and display it side by side with your original table.

● Use the Interactive teaching program 'Data handling' (from www.standards.dfes.gov.uk/primary/publications/mathematics/itps/) to display the results of class surveys. This provides some ready-made surveys and the facility to add your own data. Start with a blank bar chart and ask children in turn to click on a button to register their choices and see the chart appear before their eyes.

● Use the Line drawing tools in the interactive whiteboard software to draw two axes. Add Clip Art to display the results graphically as a pictogram. Add a title to explain what the graph shows, label the axes and include a key to show what each small picture represents.

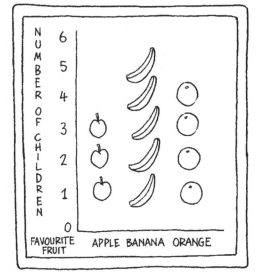

You Can... Use an interactive whiteboard to demonstrate the value of coins

Your whiteboard software should contain a full set of Clip Art pictures of different coins. These can be used in a variety of ways in mathematics lessons. Using the whiteboard allows the teacher to clearly demonstrate the value of the coins, and the whole class to be involved. The large coins make it easier to check individual children's understanding, rather than using real coins in a whole-class context. Remember that the whiteboard cannot substitute for hands-on experience, and that children will benefit from handling real coins as well as seeing them on the whiteboard.

Thinking points

● Remember to frame questions carefully and to use both open and closed questions and precise mathematical vocabulary: for example, *Are their other ways of making 20p using different coins? How many different ways can you make 10p? What silver coin has the largest value?*

● Reinforce the fact that children need to look at the number on the coin to find its value, and not count the quantity of coins.

● Plan to incorporate a range of coin-recognition activities as mental starters. Exchanging coins for different amounts also offers potential as a whole-class introduction using the whiteboard, followed by a main activity in which children use real coins to complete a similar task.

● Two of the activities right use 'characters'. Use images from the bank of Clip Art provided with your whiteboard software.

Tips, ideas and activities

● Show two characters, one with a purse containing a 20p coin, the other with an empty purse, and display a selection different coins. Ask: *How many 1p coins will make 20p?* Drag twenty 1p coins into the empty purse saying; *twenty 1p coins equal 20p.* Repeat with 2p, 5p and 10p coins, describing the calculation each time. Extend this by asking for other ways of making 20p. Demonstrate using 10p, 5p and 5p; then challenge the children to find other ways using real coins.

● Divide the class into two teams. Display a selection of coins. Describe one, for example, *It is round. It is silver. It has the smallest value of all of the silver coins.* Ask the first team to guess the coin. If they answer correctly, they drag the coin to their side of the whiteboard. Then a child from the first team describes a coin to the second team. Continue until all of the coins have been recognised. The team with the most coins wins the game.

● Display different coins and write their values beneath them. Hide each value by placing a rectangle over it using the Shape tool on your whiteboard software. Ask children to say or write each value before revealing it.

● Display your character with a purse filled with coins. Ask the children to exchange her coins to make her purse lighter.

You Can... Use an interactive whiteboard for 100 square activities

The interactive whiteboard offers an excellent way to teach place value using a 100 square. A large 100 square can easily be made using a 10 × 10 table in Microsoft Word. Rows can be made wider by pressing enter after typing in the number. This makes the 100 square 'square shaped', rather than rectangular. A 100 square can be downloaded, free of charge, from the DfES Interactive teaching programs website: http://www.standards.dfes.gov.uk/primary/publications/mathematics/itps/. Alternatively, your whiteboard software may provide ready-made 100 squares.

Thinking points
● Carefully consider the mathematical vocabulary that you plan to use, for example, 10 more, 10 less, 1 more, 1 less.

● Emphasise that counting on and back needs to be accurate, especially when moving from one row to the next.

● Consider using just part of the square on occasions to emphasise counting across the tens, or use a square with numbers from 51 to 150 to count across one hundred.

● Consider ways in which you can use different colours to visually emphasise different patterns on the 100 square.

● Give children individual 100 squares to use alongside the large 100 square on the whiteboard. Individual children can then give their answers to the whole class on the whiteboard, and explain their reasoning and understanding.

Tips, ideas and activities
● Choose a block of four numbers from the 100 square, for example:

36	37
46	47

Ask children to look at the relationship between the numbers using the correct mathematical language.

● Use the 100 square to show patterns for the 2-, 5- and 10-times tables. Use the font colour tool to change the colour of the multiples. For example, change the colour of all the multiples of 10 to red and leave the rest of the 100 square black.

● Use the 100 square to teach other counting patterns, for example, counting on and back in 1s and 10s. Change the font colour of the numbers to clearly represent the pattern.

● Use the 100 square to demonstrate addition and subtraction calculations by counting on and back in 1s. The numbers can be coloured to represent the calculation and reinforce the importance of accuracy.

● Use the 100 square to teach adding and subtracting 1′
Colour a number in red, then colour the number that ′
more in blue and the number that is 10 less in gre′
the pattern of the position of the numbers and ′
the digits in each number. Adapt the activit′
subtracting 9, 11 and other near multipl′

You Can... **Use an interactive whiteboard for number line activities**

Using a whiteboard for number line activities allows the whole class to be involved. It also enables you to clearly and visually demonstrate 'hopping' or 'jumping' between numbers, perhaps using a fun Clip Art image, such as a frog. You can create your own number line, or your whiteboard software may provide ready-made number lines. Interactive number lines can also be downloaded from the DFES Interactive teaching programs website (www. standards.dfes.gov.uk/primary/publications/ mathematics/itps/).

Thinking points

● Create your own number lines using the drawing tool in Microsoft Word or PowerPoint. Add the numbers by typing them into text boxes underneath the line and use objects from Clip Art, or the arrow tool, to move along the number line.

● Remember that your number line doesn't have to begin at 0 or 1. It could start at a 2- or 3-digit number, depending on the ages and abilities of the children.

● Children need a picture of the ordered numbers in their heads. Make sure that you use a mixture of complete, demarcated and blank interactive number lines to support children's understanding of number.

● Think about different ways in which interactive number lines can be used in your lessons: for example, counting, performing mental calculations and jotting down intermediate calculations.

Tips, ideas and activities

● Position a marker on a number line with given end points, and hide the number. Challenge children to estimate and then accurately work out what the number is, before revealing it.

● Use the number line as a visual aid to help children to count forwards and backwards. Demonstrate addition and subtraction calculations using a Clip Art frog to show the 'hops' backwards and forwards.

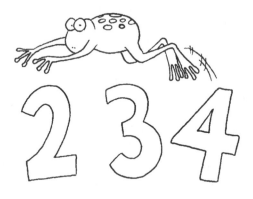

● For a quick mental starter, display an unordered number line. Ask children to drag individual number cards to the correct position and complete any missing numbers.

● Divide the class into two teams. Place Clip Art goalposts at each end of the number line. Place a Clip Art football at the centre of the number line (above number 5 on a 0 – 10 number line). Each team takes turns to roll a large dice. One team always adds the number on the dice and the other team always subtracts the number on the dice. The football is moved to the correct number each time. The team that gets the football in their goal first wins the game.

● Reinforce mathematical language such as 'the number before' and 'the number after'. Ask questions such as *What number comes in between?* using the number line to illustrate examples.

You Can... **Use an interactive whiteboard for doubling and halving**

Using shapes and Clip Art images on a whiteboard offers a useful visual tool to demonstrate doubling and halving. Prepared number lines and number squares are also useful for this purpose, as doubles and halves can easily be annotated or highlighted. You can create your own number lines and 100 squares, use those provided by your whiteboard software, or download the ones provided on the DfES Interactive teaching programs website: www. standards.dfes.gov.uk/primary/publications/mathematics/itps/

Thinking points

● When children count numbers aloud, display a large coloured 100 square on the whiteboard and point to each number as it is spoken – this will be particularly useful for children with English as an additional language and children with special needs. Exposure to the grid over time will support visual learners and encourage them to memorise patterns that will help them to recall doubles and halves (and, later, multiples and factors).

● Children will need to have an understanding of odd and even numbers before learning to halve numbers.

● Consider giving less able children or kinaesthetic learners some cubes to use whilst you are demonstrating doubling and halving on the whiteboard.

Tips, ideas and activities

● Display a small square shape and ask children to hold up one thumb. Say: *Double 1 is the same as 1 add 1*. Show another square and ask the children to hold up another thumb. Say: *Double 1 is 2*. Put the squares on top of each other. Then ask children to use their fingers to double 2. Make another two-square tower using and say: *2 + 2 = 4 and that is the same as double 2. Double 2 is 4*. Repeat for a range of doubles and halves.

● Show ten numbers and ask children to identify starting numbers and their doubles. Highlight the numbers in a specific colour or erase them as they are identified. Vary the numbers according to ability levels.

● Display a number line and ask children to say the even numbers. Tell them that they are going to halve the even numbers. Make two oval-shaped sets on the whiteboard. Make a tower using four small squares. Halve the tower by sharing the squares equally between the two sets. Say: *Half of 4 is 2*. Repeat this activity to halve all the even numbers on the number line.

● Use the constant function key of an on-screen calculator to count doubles of numbers. Challenge children to see how far they can go.

You Can... Use an interactive whiteboard to teach simple number sentences

For children to gain a better understanding of a simple addition or subtraction number sentence, it is useful for them to see objects being added to and taken away from a group. Using the Clip Art from the image bank provided by the whiteboard software, it is easy to create a visual display of objects that can be added to and taken away from. The whiteboard allows the whole class to see the demonstration clearly and then to get involved with creating a visual display of their own number sentences for others to work out.

Thinking points

● Consider using a small number of objects to begin with, as some children may have difficulties counting larger numbers without being able to physically touch or move the objects.

● Support children who are less confident by grouping the objects to be counted in fives, and arranging them like the dots on a dice.

● Ensure children are at ease with the idea of addition as combining two groups and subtraction as taking away from a group, before formal number sentences are introduced.

● Encourage more able children to show a number sentence by drawing the corresponding jump forwards or backwards along a number line.

● For the activities described in this section, create pages in the whiteboard software before the lesson with various numbers of animals already in each pen. This will save valuable time during the lesson.

● Save the pages you create for use on another occasion, for example as an oral/mental starter or for a plenary session.

Tips, ideas and activities

● Draw a large rectangle and tell the children it is an animal pen. Select a Clip Art animal, and insert several copies into the pen. Ask the children to count the animals; then write the number beneath.

● To demonstrate addition, select a different animal, and insert several copies into the pen. Ask the children to count the new animals; then demonstrate how to write the addition part of the number sentence. Ask the children to work out how many animals there are altogether; then demonstrate how to complete the number sentence beneath the pen.

● Encourage less able children to imitate what they see on the whiteboard with plastic animals.

● To demonstrate subtraction, drag some of the animals outside the pen. Ask the children to count how many animals are removed; then demonstrate how to write the subtraction part of the number sentence. Ask the children to work out how many animals are left in the pen and demonstrate how to complete the number sentence.

● Repeat the addition and subtraction activities using different numbers of animals. Ask children to write the number sentence each time.

● Let the children make number sentences of their own by dragging the animals into and out of the pen, writing the number sentence beneath.

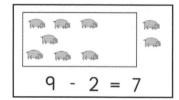

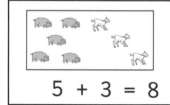

You Can... **Use an interactive whiteboard for counting and estimating**

Children begin counting by touching and moving objects. As they progress, they need to practise counting at a distance. The National Numeracy Strategy suggests counting windows, chairs and pictures on a wall. This objective can also easily be achieved by preparing sets of objects on the interactive whiteboard and challenging children to count them from a distance. Using the whiteboard adds a new dimension to teaching counting and estimating, and allows the children to count in a fun and exciting way.

Thinking points

● Follow the steps below to create a PowerPoint presentation that can be used for both counting and estimating skills:

1) Open a PowerPoint presentation and click Ctrl + N to create a new blank presentation.

2) Find Insert on the main menu. Locate Picture and select Clip Art. Type in the name of an object, animal or plant and click OK. Click on the picture you want and it will be inserted on to the page. Keep clicking on the picture until you have the number of objects you want the children to estimate or count.

3) To make the numeral appear after the children have counted, find Insert, and click Text Box. Type in the number you require and change the type size if necessary. Then right click on the text box, select Custom Animation, and in the 'Add effect' dialog box, select, for example, Fly.

Tips, ideas and activities

● If you want the children to have time to estimate the number of objects, insert a blank slide in between each picture slide, so that you can click on to the blank slide when you want to hide the objects. By clicking PgUp and PgDn, or using the up and down arrows on your keyboard, you can go back and forward in the slide show as required.

● Children often find estimating a set of objects difficult and will usually try to count the sets. When you present sets of objects for children on the whiteboard, use the whiteboard tools to hide each set after a few seconds on screen. In this way, children will learn to estimate rather than count the objects on screen.

● The presentation can be used for developing both counting and estimating skills. Add to the files as the children progress through the year. Do this by clicking on a picture and then clicking Edit, Copy, and then Edit, Paste. This will allow you to add more pictures to the screen to increase the size of the numbers. Remember to change the numeral in the text box and to save changes under a different title, so that you do not lose your original presentation.

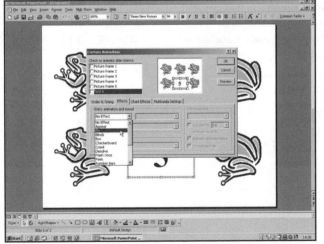

Screenshots reprinted by permission of Microsoft Corporation

You Can... Use an interactive whiteboard for investigating multiples

Children need plenty of opportunities to practise counting in multiples of 1, 2, 3, 5 and 10 in Key Stage 1. An interactive whiteboard is a great asset to help children to visualise number patterns. Patterns on 100 squares and number lines can be highlighted in memorable and striking ways. If number patterns are coloured and animated, the impact can be dramatic in terms of improving children's visualisation of multiples. Number lines and a 100 square can be downloaded, free of charge, from the DfES Interactive teaching programs website: www.standards.dfes.gov.uk /primary/publications/mathematics/itps/.

Thinking points

● Follow the steps below to prepare a PowerPoint presentation to practise counting in multiples:

1) Open a New presentation and create a blank slide by pressing Ctrl + N.

2) Find Insert on the main menu, select Picture and click on WordArt. Select an appropriate style and click on it. Type the first number in your pattern in the box and then click OK.

3) Adjust the number so that it fills the slide by clicking on the corner of the picture and dragging it.

4) Down the side of your screen there is a smaller version of the slide. Click on it so that a blue border appears. Now click Edit and Copy, then Edit and Paste. An identical slide will appear. Click on the second slide. Double click on the number and change the number to the next number in the pattern. Repeat as necessary.

Tips, ideas and activities

● Run the PowerPoint presentation you have created (see Thinking points, left). When you play the slide, each number will be revealed one at a time when the mouse is clicked. The children can count along and you (or one of the children) can control how slow or fast they go. Children can also predict the next number in the pattern.

● Save your presentation using an appropriate title, for example, 'Counting in multiples of 2'. It can then be used as a template for other similar presentations. Remember to keep a copy of the original presentation. A good idea is to save the presentation under a different title as soon as you open it and before you start to modify it. For example, you could save it as 'Counting in multiples of 5'.

● When modifying your presentation, think about changing the colour and style of the numbers or adding different sounds, to give you a range of different templates to choose from. This will help to keep the counting activities fresh and exciting.

● Use the 100 square from the DfES Interactive teaching programs to investigate multiples. Highlight different multiples on the square, or ask the children to highlight all the numbers that are multiples of 2 and look for patterns.

You Can... **Use an interactive whiteboard to create collaborative poems and rhymes**

Using an interactive whiteboard, you can create collaborative poems and rhymes, save them, and then return to and improve them later in the week. The whiteboard also allows children to focus on rehearsing their ideas, as mistakes can be deleted or changed with ease. Using a whiteboard for shared writing tasks is great for generating lots of ideas and keeping the lesson pace fast. However, it is also important that children often see you modelling the process of writing by hand, and that you talk through the process of writing.

Thinking points

● Think about font style and size. Save your choice as default by finding Format, clicking Font, then Select style and size, and click the Default option in the bottom left-hand corner.

● Explain basic ICT skills as you work, so that children learn the routine of opening new files and saving work.

● Follow the steps below to make a class rhyming bank:

1) Open a PowerPoint Presentation. Insert a text box into the first slide and write '–ad'. Make a list of '–ad' words ('mad', 'had', 'sad'). Insert pictures where appropriate. Make new slides for different 'rimes'.

2) Give the presentation a title, 'Rhyming Bank', and save it on to the class computer. It can be referred to when the class create collaborative poems or when children create their own poems.

3) Keep adding examples to the bank. This is a good activity for the word level part of the literacy hour.

Tips, ideas and activities

● Nursery rhymes provide a good starting point for discussion, since children may already be familiar with their format. Children sometimes find it easier to suggest alternatives to the rhyming words of a nursery rhyme, rather than being asked to find rhymes to words out of context.

● Talk about the poem or rhyme you want to write and ask the children for their ideas. Type in suggestions and ask children to read them aloud to check if they sound right. You could ask a classroom assistant to type as you brainstorm ideas with the children.

● Open the rhyming bank at the beginning of the lesson and minimise it (by clicking on the line in the top right-hand corner of the screen) while you type your collaborative poem. Then, whenever you are looking for a rhyme, you can click on it and look down the list for an appropriate word.

You Can... **Use an interactive whiteboard to interact with texts**

One of the obvious advantages of using an interactive whiteboard is the facility to display text on screen in any size, colour and font. It is possible to enlarge and illustrate text in a way that a photocopier or big book would never be enable you to do, and to present it as a sharp, clear image. Teachers and children can interact with the text by highlighting, editing, copying and pasting any section. A huge advantage over using conventional texts is that when a mistake is made the user can undo the previous command to remove it.

Thinking points

● Consider how much text to display. At this age, reading texts aloud from the board should be undertaken using short sequences. Use the Screen Shade or Reveal tool from the whiteboard software, if this is available, to limit the amount of text on screen at any one time.

● When using a website, consider the content of the text: is the language appropriate for the children in the class and is it aimed at a Key Stage 1 audience? Can children see the website text clearly? Do you need all of the text or just part of it?

● Consider the copyright implications before copying, pasting and manipulating any published texts. Check the front of a book or a website homepage for any restrictions before using a text in this way.

Tips, ideas and activities

● Create cloze procedure activities on the whiteboard: copy or type a text on to the board and edit out key words, such as adjectives. Then ask the class to suggest a range of alternatives.

● Enlarge text on a website by clicking on View at the top of the web browser and selecting Text Size. All web browsers automatically default to a medium view and there are usually two larger sizes available.

● Interactive texts often contain hyperlinks (coloured and underlined text that takes the user to a different document or web page). With younger children, it is unlikely that you will use these very often, but when you do, be aware that they don't divert you from the main teaching focus.

● Interact with texts to teach children to read common words by using the highlight and speech tools:
  ● Insert speech bubbles to pictures on a text using the shapes from the Drawing Toolbar.
  ● Ask children to come to the front of the class to annotate the text, to find key words and time connectives, or to change common words such as 'said' for more interesting ones.

You Can... **Use an interactive whiteboard for shared reading**

Choices of text for shared and guided reading are often limited to published big books. With an interactive whiteboard, choices become almost limitless, especially for schools with Internet access. Texts displayed electronically can be manipulated, edited or annotated, subject to any copyright restrictions. Unlike books, it is possible to save changes whilst keeping a copy of the original version. Versions of the text can also be printed off for investigation, or to be used as writing prompts.

Thinking points

● Subject to copyright, passages of texts from books can be copied and imported into programs like Microsoft Word or PowerPoint. Pictures can be scanned and placed to match the original design.

● Carefully chosen Internet pages make excellent shared texts. There are many exciting and relevant sites that offer a wide variety of text types (for example, the BBC web site, www.bbc.co.uk/schools). Use this content 'live', or copy it by clicking Print Screen and pasting into Word, copyright permitting.

● Take time to ensure the whiteboard is correctly configured, so that any annotations or marks made using the pens will be precise.

● Think about the size of the extract or web page and adjust View as required.

Tips, ideas and activities

● Control the amount of text visible with the Screen Shade or Reveal tool. This has a grab handle at the top and by dragging down using the whiteboard pen it reveals text line-by-line or paragraph-by-paragraph. This is an invaluable tool for focusing attention on each part of the text, and enables slower readers to keep up.

● Imported texts can be highlighted during a shared investigation. Click on the Highlight tool and drag it across the key words you wish to focus upon. This tool can be used in many ways: identifying use of different punctuation; locating high frequency words; identifying figurative language; finding links between paragraphs; identifying plurals; highlighting spelling patterns, for example words with a particular sound or blend. Having seen this process modelled, pages can be printed for children to investigate and highlight by hand independently.

● Use the Pen tool in different colours to note features of the text, for example connectives, as it is read. Annotation on the whiteboard is easy. Use pens to circle, underline, or draw arrows to anything on the page – words, paragraphs, headings, illustrations or captions. Also, encourage the children to come out and use the tools. Annotations can be saved, printed or removed as necessary.

You Can... **Use an interactive whiteboard to teach phonemes**

When you are introducing a new phoneme to the children, it is always useful to have pictures of objects that include that phoneme. Teachers often print or draw pictures, laminate them and store them for this purpose. With an interactive whiteboard, this process is much easier, as all the pictures can be stored on the computer. Also, the whiteboard can help you to make the activity even more interesting, for example by animating your examples.

Thinking points

● The whiteboard can be used to supplement the DfES document *Progression in Phonics* (*PiPs*), which includes a fantastic range of phonics games. Think about whether you could adapt some of the *PiPs* games for use on the interactive whiteboard.

● Do not feel that you have to replace all of the successful phonics games you already use. Always start with the question: *Can this be done more easily and effectively with a whiteboard?*

● For each new phoneme introduced, a PowerPoint Presentation can be created. Gradually, a bank of phonics presentations can be built up, which can be used year on year and adapted where necessary. The pictures will not get old, damp or ripped and can be easily supplemented where necessary.

● There are many Internet sites that contain wonderful phonic activities. BBC Words and Pictures (www.bbc.co.uk/schools/wordsandpictures/index.shtml) is one of the best.

Tips, ideas and activities

● Follow the steps below to create a PowerPoint presentation. Each slide features a picture of something that contains the phoneme being focused on, for example 'sh'. First, the children look at the picture and write the word on their individual whiteboards. Next, you click to reveal the word and the children can check their own spelling.

1) Open PowerPoint and save the presentation using an appropriate title.

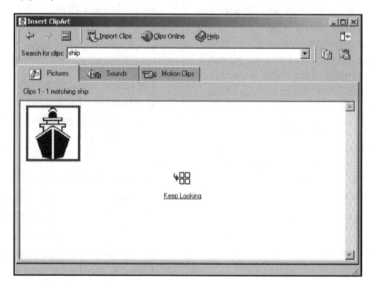

2) Type in a title for the slide, for example, 'sh_ words'

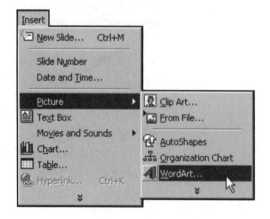

3) Insert a new slide. On to this, insert a picture or animation of a word that contains that sound, for example 'ship'. To do this, select Insert, then Picture and click on Clip Art. Type 'ship' in the Search for Clips box and select an appropriate picture or animation from the available options. Roll over the picture and select the Insert Clips icon. The picture will then appear in your PowerPoint slide.

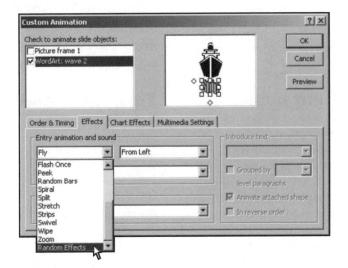

4) Now add the word. To do this, select Insert, then Picture and click on WordArt. Choose and double click on an appropriate word style, then type the word 'ship' in the Edit WordArt Text Box. Click OK (or double click) to insert the text in your PowerPoint presentation.

5) Click on the WordArt text so that a box appears around it; then drag and drop the text below the picture.

6) To animate the text so that it appears in one click after the picture, select Custom Animation from the Slide Show menu. Next select the Effects tab and choose an option from the Entry Animation box (Random Effects is a good option). To see the effect before selecting the option, click the Preview option. When you are happy, click OK to select.

7) Repeat the process on the next slide with a different picture and word. To insert a new slide select New Slide from the Insert menu.

● If you want the children to read the word rather than write it, animate the picture to appear after the word. The children can then read the word together before you reveal the picture.

You Can... # Use an interactive whiteboard to make an electronic book of children's work

Children love to see their work on display. What better motivation could there be than displaying their work in an electronic book to view on the interactive whiteboard? Children can either produce work directly on the computer to be made into an electronic book; or the work they produce in books and on paper can be scanned or photographed and inserted into an electronic book. Electronic books can be produced easily using either the software provided with your interactive whiteboard or Microsoft PowerPoint.

Thinking points

● If your scanner is located on another machine, you will need to consider how to transfer your scanned images to the whiteboard computer. Good quality scanned images can be much larger than the capacity of a floppy disk. Connecting the scanner to the computer that controls the whiteboard may be the easiest option.

● Any digital photographs taken of children's work need to be taken using a reasonably high resolution, to ensure the image is of a good quality when it is displayed.

● When evaluating work that the children have produced electronically, point out how easy it is to edit the work compared with editing a paper-based version.

● If any of the children's work is going to be displayed outside school, for example on the school website, ensure that the parent's consent has been sought.

Tips, ideas and activities

● Scan in children's artwork, based around a particular theme. Insert each of the scanned images on to a new page of the interactive whiteboard software, resizing as necessary. Ask children to name their pieces and type the name underneath the image using a keyboard.

● Use PowerPoint to create an electronic book during a shared writing session. Insert a number of pages using a template that provides space for an image on one side and a text box on the other side. Add Clip Art, photographs or children's drawings to the image box. Ask children to think of, and then type in, the appropriate text. Read and evaluate the end product and edit it accordingly.

● Ask children to work in groups to pick out their best pieces of work for a particular topic. Photograph or scan the work chosen. Insert all of the images into the interactive whiteboard software and resize them so that they can be rearranged. Let the group enhance their page further by adding some explanatory text.

● Use electronic books as a record of children's work in a particular topic and also for assessment purposes. They will look impressive on display at parent information evenings.

You Can... **Use an interactive whiteboard to teach writing skills**

In Key Stage 1, teachers are constantly reminding children to remember full stops, capital letters, question marks and so on. An effective way to demonstrate writing skills has always been to ask children to spot the deliberate mistake in a sentence that the teacher has written, or to come to the front of the class and punctuate a sentence. Both of these activities can be done easily and efficiently with a whiteboard.

Thinking points

● Create a PowerPoint presentation to teach punctuation of a sentence by following the steps below:

1) Open PowerPoint or another presentation package.

2) Insert a text box and type in a 'sentence', leaving out all the punctuation.

3) Find Insert, then select Picture and Clip Art. Use the search facility and type in an appropriate word. Select a picture or animation to illustrate the sentence.

4) On the left-hand side of the screen there is a smaller version of the slide. Click it: a blue border will appear around it. Now click Edit and then Copy.

5) Click underneath the small version of the first slide: a flashing horizontal line will appear. Now click Edit and then Paste. A copy of the slide will appear.

6) Click on the small version of the second slide to open it. Now add the punctuation.

7) Repeat the process to create as many slides as you need.

Tips, ideas and activities

● Run the slide show. There will be two slides: the first will show the 'sentence' without punctuation; the second will show the sentence punctuated correctly Show the first slide and ask children to copy the 'sentence' on to their whiteboards. They should then punctuate it. Then show the second slide. Ask children look at the punctuated version and compare it with their own attempt.

● Add pictures to the sentences to aid understanding of the text.

● Animate the punctuation, making it 'fly' in, to make the lesson more memorable.

● Add different sounds for each punctuation mark. Children will enjoy hearing the sound with the punctuation.

● Add a sound such as a clap or cheer to the punctuated slide to add some motivation to the task. To insert a sound, click Insert, Movies and Sounds. Then select sounds from the clip organiser until you find one that is appropriate. Microsoft's Clip Art and Media Gallery offers a large and varied collection of suitable pictures and animations to supplement those available through Word or your whiteboard software. This can be found at: http://office.microsoft.com/clipart/default.aspx?lc=en-gb

● Demonstrate writing by hand on the board, and demonstrate correct letter formation. Some whiteboards contain handwriting software for this purpose.

You Can... **Use an interactive whiteboard to tell stories**

The whiteboard provides an excellent way to tell stories, either to the whole class or with smaller groups in guided reading sessions. Interactive stories offer an engaging and stimulating way for children to learn to listen. They will also focus attention when children are reading extracts of a story, either individually or as a whole class. Think carefully about the extracts you use, and choose texts that will engage the children; alternatively, try creating your own interactive story!

Thinking points

● Make your own interactive story by preparing a PowerPoint presentation using text and Clip Art from the whiteboard's image bank. Images can also be inserted from a prepared file of photographs or scanned images, subject to copyright restrictions.

● Insert speech by using the Callouts option in the AutoShapes menu (access AutoShapes from the Drawing Toolbar). You can then ask individual children to read different character's lines. This offers an excellent opportunity to teach reading with expression.

● Consider how to tell the story. Will you use a 'talking book' with a voice-over telling the story? Will individual children take turns to read? Will you model the reading to the class? Will the class read altogether at certain points? How can you use the whiteboard to help children read together effectively?

● Consider using props alongside the story on the whiteboard, which will help to motivate kinaesthetic and tactile learners in particular.

Tips, ideas and activities

● Teach children about story structure by using a 'story hill'. Use Clip Art images to represent the beginning, middle and end of a story. Position the pictures at points on a hill. Show a character positioned at various points on the hill on different slides, to depict the stage the story has reached.

● Use a background picture as a starting point for a story and use puppets to tell the story. For example, display a picture of a scary wood on the whiteboard. Give the children a wolf puppet and a puppet to represent a little girl. Ask a child to begin the story. Stop at certain points to discuss with the class how the story can be improved, or what might happen next.

● Show children a sequence of pictures in the wrong order (for example, an egg hatching). Ask one child to put the pictures into a different order so that he or she can tell a story about the sequence of events. Ask other children to rearrange the pictures again to tell a different story.

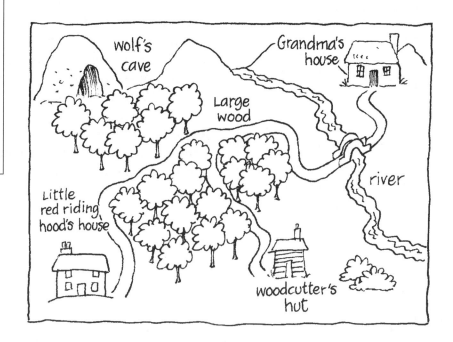

You Can... Use an interactive whiteboard to write simple sentences

The interactive whiteboard offers tremendous benefits in terms of text editing, proofreading, formulating sentences and stimulating creative writing. Parts of speech, accurate punctuation, spelling and letter formation can all be taught very effectively and in an interactive way. The whiteboard affords a range of strategies for showing best practice, modelled work and experimentation, supporting the writing process at every stage. The sheer range of possibilities, even when working with just a simple sentence, makes the interactive whiteboard an invaluable addition to any literacy lesson.

Thinking points

● Before producing a piece of text for a whole-class session, think about how it will help the children learn as well as how it will supply what you need to teach.

● When preparing sentences before a lesson, it is possible to type them using Microsoft Word and then reformat them into the whiteboard's own software (for example, '.flp' for Promethean ACTIVprimary or '.xbk' for SMART Board Notebook). In this way, text can be more easily manipulated on the whiteboard.

● It is not always necessary to create sentences from scratch – consider selecting sentences or paragraphs taken from current work, or linked to cross-curricular topics.

● Plan all of the potential uses that you could make of a piece of text and prioritise your ideas. Remember that the whole-class session should only form a small part of a well-structured and well-paced lesson.

● Make a habit of collecting pictures that will promote discussion and stimulate simple sentences.

Tips, ideas and activities

● Use the Pen or Highlighter tools to draw over and hide words in a comprehension (cloze) exercise. Use the Eraser tool to reveal the words or phrases as they are identified.

● Type or write some sentences on the whiteboard that include the word 'nice', for example; 'The nice policeman gave directions' or 'The view of the bay was very nice'. Highlight the word 'nice' and ask the children for alternatives. Annotate their suggestions on the board. This type of activity could also be used to introduce new vocabulary to replace less interesting or descriptive alternatives.

● Type a sentence and make deliberate mistakes for the children to identify.

● Type a number of sentences in the format 'Paul kicks a football'. Challenge individual children to come to the board to annotate the verbs, changing them from present tense to past or future tense. Encourage the children to write their own sentences in this format. Include some simple Clip Art from the whiteboard's image bank to stimulate interest.

● Demonstrate writing sentences on the whiteboard using the Pen tool. This tool's facility to change line width, colour and style enables clear demonstration of letter formation and makes it ideal for spelling activities linked to learning to join letters correctly.

You Can... **Use an interactive whiteboard to sequence stories**

Sequencing skills are vital in helping children to understand story structure. Instead of making and laminating sequencing cards and asking children to stick the cards in order with Blu-Tack, the same task can be created and developed using the interactive whiteboard. This activity shows you how to make an interactive activity in which the children come to the whiteboard and sequence parts of a story.

Thinking points

● The best applications to use for this activity are Microsoft PowerPoint, Publisher or the whiteboard software. Microsoft Word does not allow you to manipulate text as easily.

● The above applications allow you to add colours, backgrounds, sounds and Clip Art to your files. It is worth considering this. Although it will involve extra preparation time, once the files are created they can be saved and re-used, thus saving time in the long run.

● A similar activity can be prepared for sequencing words in a sentence.

● Back up files regularly on to a CD-ROM, memory stick or floppy disc. There is nothing more frustrating than losing all of your hard work by forgetting this basic routine.

Tips, ideas and activities

● To prepare the activity:

1) Insert a text box and type in the first sentence from the story.

2) Highlight the text and click Format and then Font. Select an appropriate font style and size. Choose a type size of at least 32 point and a child-friendly font such as Sassoon Primary or Comic Sans.

3) Put a border round the text by double clicking the text box, or right-clicking the mouse and going to Format Text Box in the drop-down menu. Change the option No Line to a colour. Repeat the process on the same slide for each sentence in the story. Use a different border colour for each text box. Drag and drop each text box into position.

● To use the activity in class, open the pre-prepared PowerPoint slide. Do not run it as a slide show because the children will not be able to move the text boxes. Close the columns on the left- and right-hand sides by clicking on the little crosses in the corners. This will make the slide bigger. Ask the children to read the sentences. Ask a child to come out and use the Pen tool to move the first text box into position. Repeat until all slides are in position.

> They liked to eat porridge for breakfast.
>
> Once upon a time there were three bears who lived in the woods.
>
> While they were out, a little girl with golden hair came walking by.
>
> Their porridge was too hot so they decided to go for a walk in the woods while it cooled down.

You Can... **Use an interactive whiteboard to create a class picture dictionary**

Demonstrating the use of a picture dictionary using the whiteboard has obvious advantages. The activity is enhanced if the children can actually be involved in making the dictionary. The resulting product will offer opportunities for teaching and learning in many areas of the literacy hour, and can also be shared with other classes. Ideally, plan the creation of the dictionary as an enjoyable extended topic over a week or longer.

Thinking points

● Consider the age and ICT skills of the children when planning your class dictionary. Both of these factors will affect the contents of the dictionary and how much involvement the children will have in producing it. If the children are unable to produce pages themselves, make sure that thinking and planning stages remain a collaborative venture.

● Although Clip Art can be used, using a digital camera in class can result in a more 'personal' class dictionary that will be more meaningful for the children.

● Taking on the whole alphabet would involve much effort over an extended period. Plan to spend a week or more of literacy time on this project, or ask the children to focus only on a few letters and build up the dictionary over a period of time.

● To create the dictionary, open a new PowerPoint presentation. Select a blank slide. Find Insert and select Picture and WordArt. Type 'Aa' in a suitable WordArt style. Click OK and then if necessary click on the text and move it into a suitable position on the slide. Insert a new slide and repeat for each letter of the alphabet.

Tips, ideas and activities

● Show the children alphabet books and explain that you are going to create a class alphabet book on the whiteboard.

● Ask the children for ideas for each page.

● Ask the children to take pictures of objects beginning with the letter 'a' with a digital camera. Transfer these to the class computer, saving them to an accessible directory.

● Open the 'Aa' page , select Insert, choose Picture and then the Picture from File option. Select a picture. Click Insert and move the picture into position using the mouse.

● Add a text box (click Insert, Text Box) and add a name label for the object, for example, 'Apple'.

● Show the presentation again and ask the children to write a definition of the word.

A type of fruit

● Look at the definitions during the plenary session, or as a shared writing activity, and choose some to add to the presentation: select a slide, click Insert, Text Box and ask a child to type in the text.

● Revisit the presentation with the children periodically, to edit and improve each letter.

● Show the dictionary to another class. Show slides with pictures only, to discuss alternative definitions; or show the pictures with definitions, and ask the children to discover the matching picture.

You Can... # Use an interactive whiteboard to link scientific effects

Work on the interactive whiteboard cannot, of course, replace the experience of practical science investigations. However, it does offer you the opportunity to demonstrate scientific effects that would otherwise be too difficult or time-consuming for the children to experience first-hand. You can use the interactive whiteboard to introduce a concept, expand upon what children have learned in the practical lesson, or consolidate, recap or assess children's learning.

Thinking points

● Think about how you will use the interactive whiteboard in your science lessons. It is important that the children experience scientific effects first-hand, for example, the effect of light and water on cress seeds; the effect of heat on substances; the effect of pushing or pulling an object. However, a whiteboard can be very useful to consolidate children's knowledge, recap previous lessons and assess children's learning.

● Prepare digital photographs to show scientific effects. For example, take photographs, at different stages, of cress seeds growing, or take photographs of different substances before and after they have been heated.

● Explore the Internet to find resources to use on the whiteboard remembering to check for any copyright restrictions. The BBC schools website has a variety of interactive experiments for Key Stage 1. Search for a wide range of images to illustrate pushing and pulling; huskies pulling a sledge, for example, or Egyptian slaves pulling blocks to build the pyramids.

Tips, ideas and activities

● The QCA Scheme of Work for Science Unit 1B: Growing plants, includes a cress seed experiment. Two plates of cress seeds are placed in the dark and two in the light. One plate in the dark and one in the light are given water. The children predict what will happen to the seeds. This teaches the children the effect of water and light on seeds. Use the interactive whiteboard to display an interactive simulation or video of this experiment. A video showing germinating cress seeds can be accessed through www.espresso.co.uk (for subscribers only). Alternatively, take digital photos of the cress seeds at various stages of germination to make a PowerPoint Slide Show, demonstrating how the seeds grow and change.

● Take digital pictures of substances before and after they have been heated or frozen. Insert the pictures into a PowerPoint presentation and use for whole-class discussion.

● The BBC website includes an activity showing the effects of pushing and pulling a toy horse on wheels (www.bbc.co.uk/schools/scienceclips/ages/5_6/pushes_pulls.shtml). It also shows what happens when obstacles are placed in the way. Show the video to encourage children to make predictions and to generate discussion.

● Source, download (copyright permitting) and present pictures of more unusual pulling and pushing activities such as a strong man pulling a train. Encourage debate about the forces present, using the Pen or Arrow tools to highlight these forces.

You Can... **Use an interactive whiteboard for sorting and classifying**

Using an interactive whiteboard provides a simple, yet visually stimulating way to sort and classify plants, animals and materials. There are a wealth of images available in Clip Art, or you can use scanned or digital photographs and simple shapes. Both the SMART Board and the Promethean ACTIVboard software provide a vast array of themed image resources within their image banks. These images can be displayed on the whiteboard and sorted into Venn or Carroll diagrams, or a branching database using branching database software or the whiteboard software.

Thinking points

● Be clear about the scientific concepts you are teaching and decide upon the most appropriate method of sorting. For example, you could use a Carroll diagram, Venn diagram or a branching database.

● Remember the importance of practical science investigations. The whiteboard should not be used to replace these. Consider how to use the whiteboard effectively alongside a practical science lesson.

● Check whether your whiteboard includes the resources that you need. It might be necessary to search the Internet or provide your own photographic images for particular subject areas, for example, sorting rocks.

Tips, ideas and activities

● Ask children to come to the board to sort images into sets and then to label the sets accordingly. Encourage the children to think of their own sets. Use images of:

● living organisms ('Wings'/'No wings'; 'Four legs'/'Eight legs')

● objects made of different materials (sort by type of material, or 'Natural' and 'Manufactured')

● different foods ('Vegetables', 'Meat', 'Dairy', or 'Healthy' and 'Unhealthy').

● Have a practical lesson sorting materials with magnetic and non-magnetic properties. On the whiteboard, display two sets ('Magnetic' and 'Non-magnetic') and text labels of the different materials. Sort the labels into the two sets as part of the plenary session. Link the activity to the children's practical work and ask them to make some statements, for example, 'Iron is magnetic but most other metals aren't.'

● Use words or Clip Art images of objects that float and sink. Test each object practically, using a container of water (positioned well away from the whiteboard). Then sort the words and pictures into sets as part of the plenary session.

● Prepare a model for a simple branching database. Create a series of yes/no questions around a theme, for example, minibeasts. Demonstrate how to carefully frame questions with yes/no answers – for example, 'Does the animal have six legs?'

You Can... Use an interactive whiteboard with a digital microscope

Children are fascinated by microscopes. The interactive whiteboard affords an opportunity to engage the whole class in an experience that makes everyone feel like a 'real' scientist. As well as developing observation skills, widening children's knowledge of real applications of ICT and allowing them to see things in a whole new light, working with a digital microscope is also great fun! Children can also be encouraged to feed back to the class using the microscope and whiteboard, to develop skills in speaking and listening.

Thinking points

- If you haven't used the microscope before, spend time exploring its functions and software before presenting it to the class.

- Choose a couple of ICT 'whizz-kids' and allow them time to 'play' with the microscope. They will soon become experts and invaluable assistants!

- Make sure children understand that although a large image is projected on the whiteboard, the object under the microscope is very small!

- Consider how the appearance of objects changes and ask questions such as: *What will this strand of hair look like when it is magnified 200 times?*

- When changing the focus on the microscope, remember that it can take a moment for the computer to catch up.

- Using the microscope as a camera and a movie-maker, or for time-lapse photography, provides excellent opportunities for scientific investigation and some obvious links to literacy and numeracy.

Tips, ideas and activities

- Show children's skin at different magnifications. Take the microscope off its stand and use it at different angles to show different body parts such as the inside of an ear or a mouth. Ensure children understand that it is the magnification of the objects that changes, not the object itself.

- Study a tooth, looking at its structure and observing the effects of decay when it is dropped in a fizzy drink. Test different types of drink.

- Use the 'movie-maker' function of the microscope to classify, observe and record the behaviour of minibeasts. Carefully count the number of legs and body parts.

- Compare a range of fabrics. Encourage children to look carefully and compare the way that the fibres make up the piece of cloth. Do this to introduce a practical experiment testing a range of fabrics to find out which is the most hardwearing, most transparent or best to protect skin from sunlight.

- Set the microscope on a fixed interval setting to take photographs of cress seeds germinating. Use the software to produce a short film showing changes in the initial stages of germination over a period of time.

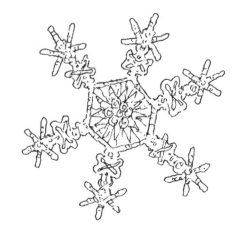

- Snow, if available, is fascinating to look at under the microscope.

You Can... **Use an interactive whiteboard to investigate sound**

Recording sound is a quick and easy process with the whiteboard. Sound recordings take up little memory and are an ideal, transportable resource for use in a computer suite or with the whole class on the whiteboard PC. All computers come pre-installed with a number of programs that record sound. In order to record, you will need either a webcam or a standard microphone: both options are inexpensive and offer a good standard of quality of sound.

Thinking points

● Consider the flexibility of your classroom set-up. Often the small microphones provided as part of the computer bundle can't pick up noise from further than 1m. If the subject is not within this range, the recording of the investigation might be lost. Also, if the subject cannot move – for example, a large instrument – then you may need to use either a PDA or laptop for the sound recording.

● To use the recording facility:

1) Click Start and then Programs.

2) Click Accessories (usually found at the top of the My Programs file) and then scroll down to Entertainment.

3) Locate the Sound Recorder icon.

4) Open the program (a small grey rectangle with a record button). Place the microphone or webcam as near to the subject as possible (this may be easier using a laptop) and press Record. The program will allow 60 seconds of recording time, which is usually sufficient.

Tips, ideas and activities

● The BBC website offers online resources on sound for Key Stage 1 children (www.bbc.co.uk/schools/scienceclips). Online models work best as a stimulus to show how the experiment would work under ideal circumstances (not often found in the primary classroom!). However, they are no substitute to actually doing the experiment.

● Save your files and store them, so that you can reuse the sounds you have recorded.

● The Sound Record program automatically displays the sound waves from the recording. This may not be part of your teaching objective but it offers a worthwhile teaching point. Use this facility for investigations on 'pitch', playing and recording a range of musical instruments. Play back the sounds to the whole class on the whiteboard and encourage each child to describe the pitch or volume of each instrument using appropriate vocabulary.

Screenshots reprinted by permission of Microsoft Corporation

Accessories	▶	Entertainment	▶	CD Player
Adobe	▶	Calculator		Sound Recorder
SnagIt	▶	Windows Explorer		Volume Control
StuffIt Standard	▶	☰		Windows Media Player
Microsoft Outlook				
Microsoft PowerPoint				
Microsoft Word				
Ahead Nero	▶			
Extensis	▶			
☰				

● Another use is to record children's comments on investigations for review and assessment purposes. Children in particular find recordings a useful tool for evaluation of work they have done.

You Can... **Use an interactive whiteboard to explain scientific words**

Using pictures and text on an interactive whiteboard is an ideal way to help children learn scientific words. The whiteboard provides an easily accessible visual aid that can be used throughout a science lesson. Both Promethen ACTIVboard and SMART Board software offer a wide range of Clip Art images that can then be labelled. Images can be drawn from other sources, such as books and websites (subject to copyright restrictions), that will also be suitable for the vocabulary you want to introduce. Video clips that explain scientific processes provide a further opportunity for consolidation of key concepts, and are particularly useful for more visual learners.

Thinking points

● Ensure images match the related word and are used appropriately. Clip Art images can be pasted on the whiteboard and labelled using the arrows from the Drawing Toolbar and text boxes. For example, label the 'leaves', 'flower', 'stem', and 'roots' of a plant, or label different body parts of a human body.

● Consider how to make the task interactive. For example, rather than pre-labelling your Clip Art image, children could be asked to drag and position the labels during the lesson.

● Frame questions carefully, to ensure children can answer using the correct vocabulary on the screen. To assess individual children's understanding, ask them to write their answers on individual whiteboards.

Tips, ideas and activities

● Ask children to use new words in a sentence, or highlight them in a text extract and explain their meanings.

● Use a video clip to explain a scientific process and pause it so that correct words can be reviewed and questions asked.

● Prepare a cloze procedure text, covering up the key scientific words. Read it and ask children to choose the correct scientific word. Reveal the word to check if they are correct.

● Make a concept cartoon using pictures from Clip Art and the speech bubble tool from the Drawing Toolbar or image library. For example, show a child standing by a tank of water and a piece of wood. Add a speech bubble: *I think it will sink because it is too large.* Reinforce the words 'floating' and 'sinking' and ask children if the child is correct.

● Make text boxes containing key words on one side of the page, and text boxes containing their explanation on the other side of the page. Ask children to link them using the arrow from the Drawing Toolbar.

● Demonstrate making a concept or mind map. List the key words. Use the arrow from the Drawing Toolbar to link ideas. Insert appropriate pictures from Clip Art.

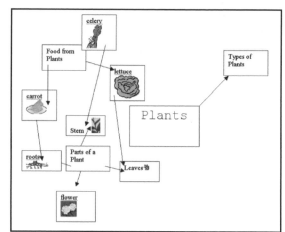

You Can... **Use an interactive whiteboard to investigate how the body works**

In the Foundation Stage and Key Stage 1, children learn about senses, body parts and how the body changes as we grow. The interactive whiteboard can be an invaluable tool in this area, because with it you can create an expandable file of pictures and information. The topic can be taught very effectively using this resource. If you already use video clips to teach how the body works, these can also be played through your whiteboard, to generate effective whole-class discussions.

Thinking points

● Think about the whiteboard tools that you might use to highlight parts of the body and your choice of media to teach the five senses. Don't forget the facility to record sound when planning lessons on the senses.

● Explore the Internet for suitable images and also video clips and presentations to do with the senses and the body.

● Remember to check the copyright restrictions for using images on an interactive whiteboard before downloading and scanning them.

● Remember to ask permission from the parents before taking and scanning photographs of children, and delete files after use.

Tips, ideas and activities

● Make a PowerPoint presentation to teach the five senses to Year 1:

1) Open a PowerPoint presentation and click New Slide.

2) Find Insert and select Picture, then Clip Art. Find a suitable picture of a face or head. Double click the picture to select and input it into your presentation.

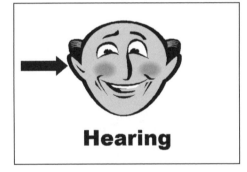

Hearing

3) Find Insert again, and then Text Box. Type 'hearing' into the text box. Find Format and Font to select an appropriate font style and size.

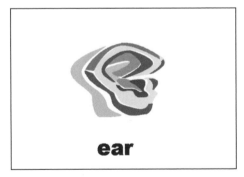

ear

4) Insert an arrow pointing to the ear. To do this, find the AutoShapes option on the Drawing Toolbar and select an arrow from the Block Arrows option. Move both the arrow and the text box into position.

5) Animate the text box by selecting Slide Show and Custom Animation. In the Add Effects dialog box, select an appropriate effect so that the text box appears after the picture and the arrow.

6) To focus further on words relating to hearing, add another slide and insert a picture of an ear and a text box with 'ear' typed in.

7) Repeat for all the other four senses.

8) When you run the show, discuss each sense and combine the presentation with songs and rhymes. Ask questions about where the sense organs are located in the body and what their functions are. Use the presentation to focus attention and assess children's understanding. The same approach can be used for parts of the body.

● Prepare a PowerPoint presentation to show Year 2 how the body changes as we grow.

1) Collect photos of yourself that show you as a baby, toddler, teenager and adult. Scan these into your computer and save them to an accessible folder.

2) Open a New presentation. Find Insert, and select Picture and From File. Insert a text box, for example, 'Mrs Jones aged 1'. Format the text box using an appropriate style and font.

3) Animate the text box to appear after the photo (see page 43).

4) Repeat the process for the other photos.

5) When you run the show, the photos will appear without text. Ask the children questions such as who they think the baby is, or how old the child is. Click the mouse to reveal the text box.

6) At the end of the show ask children how they think people change as they get older. Record on the whiteboard any observations and simple comparisons that the children are able to identify.

● Ask the children to bring in photos of themselves as babies, scan them and display them on the whiteboard. Challenge the children to guess who everyone is and discuss how they themselves have changed in just a few years.

You Can... Use an interactive whiteboard to show growing plants and animals

A whiteboard is a great way to show pictures and animations. This is useful when showing children how plants and animals grow. If you can get hold of a video clip of growing plants or animals, then this can be played through your whiteboard. The Internet has some excellent resources, which are worth taking time to explore. You can either use ready-made presentations, or alternatively prepare your own. Once you have taken the time to make these files, you will have a wonderful resource to use every year. Remember to save your files, and back them up regularly.

Thinking points

- The Internet has ready-made resources to use on the whiteboard. Look on the BBC schools website (www.bbc.co.uk/schools/scienceclips/ages/5_6/growing_plants.shtml) for an activity in which the children are asked to provide water and light to make a plant grow.

- Prepare your own presentation about growing plants and animals following the instructions given below. The Internet is a rich source of animal and plant images but you must check copyright when downloading or scanning pictures. Where possible, try to find copyright-free images. You could also use Clip Art, pictures you or the children have drawn, or photographs of the different stages taken with the children during a practical investigation.

- Locate appropriate animal sound files – these will add yet another dimension to the lesson.

- When creating a PowerPoint presentation, add an extra slide at the beginning and use it to type in the lesson objective. You can refer back to this at the end of the lesson.

Tips, ideas and activities

- Make a PowerPoint presentation to show growing plants:

    1) Open a New presentation. Find Insert, and select Picture and From File. Locate and insert a picture of a seed, then a picture of a shoot, and so on.

    2) If you want the children to sequence the pictures themselves, insert the pictures on to the same slide. (Do not open the PowerPoint presentation as a slide show because the children will not be able to move the pictures around.)

    3) Ask children to move the pictures on the whiteboard into the correct order.

    4) Print out the original slide as a worksheet and the children can cut out the pictures and sequence them in their books as an activity or assessment.

- Make a PowerPoint presentation to show how animals change as they grow:

    1) Open PowerPoint and make a title slide: 'Whose baby am I?'

    2) Insert a baby animal picture from Clip Art or another source and insert a text box underneath with the name of the baby animal, for example, 'lamb'.

    3) Insert a new slide and insert a picture of the baby's mother.

    4) When you run the show, reveal the baby, ask questions about the mother and then click to the next slide to reveal the answer.

You Can... **Use an interactive whiteboard with a webcam**

Webcams have been around for several years but they are only now coming into their own as a useful resource in the classroom. Although webcams are not a standard attachment to the interactive whiteboard, they are very simple to install. Webcams are designed as a low-end filming tool, so neither the sound nor the picture quality is of a particularly high standard. However, if you are willing to accept this, it is possible to create some interesting and interactive lessons using the webcam.

Thinking points

● Webcams have only a very basic pixel ratio but they are nevertheless ideal for sharing or 'web conferencing' scientific investigations.

● To use the webcam:

1) Access your webcam either in the bottom right-hand corner of the Toolbar or in My Computer. Find the correct drive and double-click it – it will usually display a camera or video recorder to represent the webcam.

2) Focus the webcam on the object you wish to film. Set the camera to take a photograph at regular intervals, such as every two hours.

3) Display the resulting photographs on the whiteboard.

● Check that your school's firewall will not prevent you from connecting with another user. Contact your technician for further support.

● Sound echoes may mean that your echo settings are too high. Look in the View folder to change these settings. If there is feedback, move the speakers away from the microphone. Feedback can be eliminated by using a microphone headset, though this can only be used by one person at a time.

Tips, ideas and activities

● Link photographs taken with the webcam to practical work on reversible and irreversible changes or changing states. For example, use the webcam to monitor materials changing over time, for example ice melting into water, or plants growing or wilting.

● Link photographs taken with the webcam to work on data collection. For example, use the webcam to observe the different species that visit the school bird table, and ask children to keep a record.

● Use the webcams for web conferencing. The larger messaging groups (Yahoo and Microsoft Network) offer video conferencing alongside their instant messaging and email communications.

● Use the webcam as a conference tool with another class or school. The number of frames per second that can be generated will be reliant on the speed of your Internet connection. If your

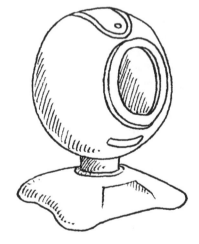

school is using broadband, the camera will run at around 20 - 30 frames per second. This will produce a video-like image, though there is often a sound delay.

You Can... **Use an interactive whiteboard to label parts of plants and animals**

A whiteboard is a great way to store and display pictures of materials, plants and animals for a variety of purposes. You can use the Clip Art resources provided with your whiteboard software, images from websites and published books (dependent on copyright restrictions), digital or scanned photographs, or drawings made by you or the children. The pictures can be downloaded or scanned, and then saved on file without any fear of them being lost or damaged. The images can be easily accessed, displayed and manipulated using the whiteboard.

Thinking points

● Always check any copyright restrictions when downloading images from the Internet or scanning pictures from books. The BBC schools website (www.bbc.co.uk/schools/ scienceclips) has some excellent activities on the subject of plants and animals.

● When preparing a lesson using multiple images or flipchart pages, add an extra slide or page at the beginning and type in the lesson objective. This can be referred back to at the end of the lesson with the question: *What have we learned today?*

● A bank of text and images can be made for every year group, gradually adding more details and probing questions to provide progression through the school.

● The same slide show can be referred to several times during the science topic and used as a revision aid. Some slides might also be printed and used as worksheets.

Tips, ideas and activities

● Use PowerPoint to create labelled pictures of plants and animals:

1) Download your chosen image by right-clicking on it. Then click Save As, giving the picture an appropriate name. Alternatively, draw a picture yourself or ask the children to draw one. Scan and save the images into the computer.

2) Open a new PowerPoint presentation. Click Insert, then Picture, then From File and find the saved picture. Insert the picture and move it into position. Enlarge it to fill most of the slide.

3) Insert a text box and type in text for the label. Highlight the word with your mouse and select an appropriate font size and style. Move the label into position, slightly away from the stem.

4) Add an arrow from the Drawing Toolbar or from AutoShapes. Click on the arrow icon and select an appropriate arrow. Move the arrow into position. Repeat for each label and arrow.

● Animate labels so that they arrive on a click:

1) Click on the label you want to animate. Click Slide Show, then Custom Animation, Effect Entrance and select an appropriate entrance; Random Effects is usually quite fun.

2) Animate the arrows in the same way. Alternatively, leave them as prompts: ask children what they think each part is called and then reveal the answer with a click.

You Can... **Use an interactive whiteboard to demonstrate pushes and pulls**

Demonstrating pushes and pulls has always been a lively, practical activity. Teachers will usually take the children outside to push and pull scooters or bicycles, or find objects to push and pull in the classroom. The interactive whiteboard should not be used to replace this invaluable hands-on experience. It can, however, help you to provide experience of, and demonstrate, pushes and pulls on objects that are not so easily accessible.

Thinking points

● There is no substitute for hands-on experience. Children need to experience pushing and pulling objects themselves on a variety of surfaces and slopes, and to identify the similarities and differences between the movement of different objects.

● Explain to the children why it is dangerous to try to stop some moving objects. Extend the discussion to road safety using a video or a CD-ROM. These can be played through an interactive whiteboard, with key learning points written or highlighted on the board.

● The BBC schools website includes an activity in which children are asked to make predictions about the effect on a toy horse if it is given a hard or soft push or pull, and if obstacles are put in its way (www.bbc.co.uk/schools/scienceclips/ages/5_6/pushes_pulls.shtml).

● Alternatively, make your own PowerPoint presentation to discuss pushes and pulls. This will enable you to show things that are not available or accessible in the school environment.

Tips, ideas and activities

● Create a pushing and pulling PowerPoint slide show:
1) Open PowerPoint and type the objective into the title slide.

2) Insert a new blank slide and insert a picture of something that can be pushed or pulled. For example, you could show a person pushing a pram.

3) Select Slide Show and Custom Animation. In the Add Effects dialog box, select Fly Out. Select To Right on the Direction drop-down menu and Slow on the speed drop-down menu (where available).

4) Run the Slide Show. You will see the person pushing the pram. Ask the children if the person is pushing or pulling the pram. Which direction will the pram move? Now click the mouse and watch the person push the pram to the right.

5) Add a new slide and add another image of an object that can be pushed or pulled, for example a lawnmower, a vacuum cleaner, a tug of war or a wheelbarrow.

6) Make an assessment activity with the pictures you collect. Put them all on to one slide and number them. Put the slide on the screen and ask the children to write the number or word in their book and write whether it demonstrates a push or a pull.

You Can... **Use an interactive whiteboard to look at objects from the past**

An interactive whiteboard enables objects to be displayed as large colour images on the screen, so that the whole class can discuss them. If you build up a collection of pictures of historical artefacts, it is even possible to create your own 'virtual museum'. Many older resources can be revamped, and a scanner is invaluable for importing favourite pictures. Remember to check the copyright restrictions on the images that you use on your whiteboard.

Thinking points

● There are an increasing number of electronic big books dedicated to the QCA units of work for History. Many of these are rich in images and explanatory text and are well worth exploring.

● Think about how the pictures of objects will be used on the whiteboard. You might highlight (or spotlight) features of the object, organise the pictures in a presentation, resize them for ease of use or annotate them in order to pick out key features.

● It is important to share your virtual museum with other classes, promoting speaking and listening skills across the school.

● Taking digital photos of old toys that children bring in means that the toys only need to stay at school for one day and so are less likely to get damaged.

Tips, ideas and activities

● Invite parents and grandparents in to discuss their favourite toys as part of a wider QCA project on 'Toys'. Encourage these guest speakers to describe the toys and how they played with them. If they can bring in the toys, photograph them and display them on the whiteboard in your virtual museum.

● If possible, record the voice of each guest speaker and incorporate the resulting sound files into your virtual museum's slide show presentation. To do this plug a microphone into the computer. Click Start, then Programs, and find Accessories, Entertainment and finally Sound Recorder. Record the speaker and save to a suitable location. Next, insert the saved file into the relevant PowerPoint slide showing the toy that the speaker was describing.

● When you run the show, start by asking children for their ideas on what each toy is and how it works. Then, click on the sound icon and the sound file will play.

● Collect small artefacts like coins, jewellery or stamps. Share them with the whole class using the whiteboard. Take digital photographs of the images and enlarge them, or place each object in the viewing tray of a digital microscope so that the whole class can see in detail.

You Can... **Use an interactive whiteboard to look at life in past times**

Children often regard the past as unimportant because they perceive that people and events from earlier times don't affect them. Sources of evidence often tell us the 'what, when, where and who', but seldom inform us about people's emotional responses to historical events. The interactive whiteboard can become a 'window' on the past, developing children's understanding of, and empathy with, people from long ago. Well-chosen historical images can help generate discussion on the lives of people from the past. Such discussions can then be extended into drama or creative writing activities. Remember to check copyright restrictions on images you use on the whiteboard.

Thinking points

- Start collecting historical photographs to show on the whiteboard. These are available to buy in packs and can be copied from books or the Internet (copyright permitting), for example from virtual museums.

- Look for sound archives on the Internet to play to the class and play excerpts from historical films and documentaries. Check that your whiteboard PC includes a DVD software player (such as Cyberlink PowerDVD Player).

- Consider inviting a grandparent into school, to discuss their early life. If this cannot be arranged, video an interview with an older person or link a webcam to the whiteboard and interview someone from an older generation via a video link.

Tips, ideas and activities

- Two useful history websites are:
  1) www.britishpathe.com, which provides free film resources from the past. To show these on the whiteboard you will need a reasonably fast Internet connection. The films contain a wealth of information about how people lived before, during and after World War 2 – in particular, the experience of children who were evacuated during the War.

  2) www.bbc.co.uk/schools provides useful and interesting activities (follow the history links for 4-11 year olds).

- Select the 'history' hyperlink to find links to topics such as famous people, Dynamo's History, Anglo Saxons, Children of War, Romans, Vikings, Celts and Victorians.

- Scan (or copy) photographs which are not restricted by copyright and present them as slide shows or insert them into programs like PowerPoint, providing a large, bold and vivid focus for the whole class.

- Scan (or copy) text extracts, again remembering to check for any copyright restrictions. During shared reading, highlight emotive descriptions or imagery on the whiteboard.

- Use the whiteboard as a basis for discussion about how the way people lived in the past is different from the way we live today. It is always interesting to discover children's views and ideas, and these sometimes give rise to unexpected observations.

- Create a piece of collaborative writing to help children understand people's situations from different perspectives.

You Can... Use an interactive whiteboard to investigate the local area

An interactive whiteboard can bring the local area into the classroom by enabling you to display local maps and photographs on a large scale, for all children to see clearly. The whiteboard makes it possible to annotate photographs and maps without the originals being damaged or even touched by the children. The drag and drop facility built into the software provided by the whiteboard allows smaller images of features within the area to be sorted in a variety of ways. The children's spatial awareness can be developed using maps and aerial photographs.

Thinking points

● The whiteboard is no substitute for practical experience. Go on a class walk around the local area at the start of the topic to give them a chance to notice the less obvious features. Make sure that the investigation is relevant to the children. For example, if there is a drive to encourage more children to walk to school, ensure your investigation considers transport to school.

● Digital photographs of specific places or features around the area can be really useful to help the children to visualise what is being discussed. When taking digital photographs to use on the interactive whiteboard, consider how large you need the pictures to be and set the camera resolution accordingly. Photographs displayed on a full screen will need a high resolution to give a good quality image. For smaller photographs, which will be dragged around the screen, a low resolution will be adequate.

Tips, ideas and activities

● Display digital photographs of the local area by inserting them into the interactive whiteboard software. Discuss the features in the photographs and ask the children to label them.

● Place a variety of small photographs of local features into the interactive whiteboard software. Split the page in half using the line drawing tool and label one side 'Human features' and the other side 'Physical features'. Discuss the meanings of these terms with the children and then ask them to drag and drop the photographs into the correct half of the page.

● Scan a map or aerial photograph of the local area into the computer, remembering to check for copyright restrictions, and insert it into the interactive whiteboard software. Show the children where the school and features of the area are. Ask them to find their own house 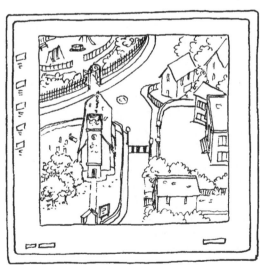 or other features, such as the local park. Use a whiteboard pen to draw the children's routes to and from school.

● Carry out a survey of the traffic passing by the school gates, or the ways in which children travel to school. Chart the results of the survey using Microsoft Excel or the Numeracy Strategy's Interactive teaching program on data handling, which can be found on the DfES Standards website (www.standards.dfes.gov.uk/primary/publications/mathematics/itps/).

You Can... **Use an interactive whiteboard to see the world**

The term World Wide Web clearly suggests the wide reach of the Internet and the wealth of resources it can access. From tourist websites to radio and television news sites, it is possible to view information and images from any country in the world. Such resources can easily be displayed on the whiteboard, or used to create your own PowerPoint presentations to show slides of landscapes and landmarks, or to look at local or global maps. Remember to check for any copyright restrictions before using pictures and maps from websites or published materials.

Thinking points

● Consider which aspect of a country's culture is being studied. Define your search criteria and use search engines, such as www.google.co.uk or www.yahoo.co.uk, to find the information you are looking for.

● Click on the Image Only button (usually located next to the Search Box) if you only want to locate images from websites, rather than the websites themselves.

● Visit your chosen country's tourist information. It might also be possible to view a webcam attached to places of local interest.

● Ask children to bring in pictures of your chosen location from magazines or tourist brochures, to scan and use on the whiteboard.

● Check whether your school or LEA have an international link or 'twinning' partnership. If so, develop the links between children through email, digital photo swaps, webcam video links or file sharing.

Tips, ideas and activities

● Make a presentation about another country and add Action Buttons that link to websites, pictures of landmarks and sound files of local music. Select Slide Show and Action buttons. Then choose from a range of buttons, including an Information button, Video button or Sound button. This can be used to support the QCA Scheme of Work for Geography Unit 5: Where in the World is Barnaby Bear?

● Use the same idea in a presentation about the local area. Prepare a PowerPoint map of the local area and then take digital photos of local landmarks. Add Action Buttons to the map that link to photos of the various locations. This work can be used to support QCA Scheme of Work for Geography, Unit 1: Around our school.

● Use the Drawing or Pen tools to label and highlight features on photographs and invite children to add their own comments or annotations.

You Can... **Use an interactive whiteboard to investigate food from round the world**

'Food around the world' is a topic that links science, geography and citizenship. The use of electronic resources on the interactive whiteboard can bring this topic to life and will help to answer a range of questions such as: Where does our food come from? How is it grown? *and* What do children in other countries eat?

Thinking points

● Check that your interactive whiteboard computer has access to the Internet. If it doesn't, it would be worth investing in it: without an Internet connection, you and your colleagues will only be able to access a very small proportion of the whiteboard's capabilities, particularly when studying other the food and culture of other countries.

● Decide which countries to study. Choose contrasting countries, such as China, Italy and India. You could link the lesson with a data-handling activity by conducting a survey to find out what foods from other countries are eaten by children in the school – for example, curry, pizza and paella.

● Set the children some questions to answer, for example: *Does everyone in the world eat the same things? What is the same/different?* Use this work to establish connections between different countries, their cultures and their lifestyles. Set this work in the wider context of a project or topic about food.

Tips, hints and activities

● Display a map of the world and highlight the countries you will be investigating. Save a map of each country to a PowerPoint presentation. Use these as the centrepiece of an interactive poster about each country and its food.

● Ask children to research the food eaten in the selected countries: how it is grown and how it is transported. Ask children to identify websites and bring in pictures, for example of rice being cultivated or bananas being picked. Scan the pictures (taking account of any copyright restrictions) and add them to the presentation. Add Action Buttons to link the pictures and information to the maps.

● Ask children to investigate what types of food from different cultures are popular in this country. They could show examples of different foods on supermarket websites or bring in examples from home for a whole-class display. Take a photograph of the display to use in your interactive poster.

● Ask children about their favourite foods or which foods from around the world they would like to try. Make a whole-class pictogram or tally chart of the class results. Find suitable Clip Art for the pictogram, or scan in pictures of each item.

You Can... **Use an interactive whiteboard to explore colour, size and shape**

You can produce some very striking designs and patterns using simple graphics packages such as Paint. When creating pictures using Paint, there is no fear of committing anything to paper. Any mistakes can be quickly undone without the tell-tale marks of an eraser. The children can also use the tools to create different shapes in different sizes. They can then change the colour, producing completely different works of art. Use the interactive whiteboard to demonstrate techniques and to review children's work.

Thinking points

● Explore the whiteboard's drawing tools. Most offer a range of pen and highlighter tools. You should also be able to modify the thickness and colour of drawing objects and the background colour of the screen.

● Follow these instructions to set up a sorting activity using Microsoft Publisher or Word:

1) Click Table and then Insert table.

2) Select four columns and two rows.

3) Give each column a heading: 'Green shapes with less than four sides'; 'Red shapes with less than four sides'; 'Green shapes with four or more sides'; 'Red shapes with four or more sides'.

4) Go to the Drawing Toolbar and find AutoShapes. Select a shape and double click on it. Change its colour to green or red.

5) Repeat until you have enough shapes and position them under the table.

6) Adjust the size of the table if necessary by clicking on the square in the bottom right-hand corner.

Tips, ideas and activities

● Display the pre-prepared table and ask children to move each shape into its correct location. Adapt the activity for different levels of ability. Print it out as a follow-up worksheet activity, for the children to cut and stick. Prepare a completed version to show on the whiteboard at the end of the lesson.

● Graphics packages are best used to draw simple patterns and abstract drawings using a variety of techniques, rather than drawing complex, fine line pictures. Ask children to create a repeating pattern using the Shape tools in Paint. They can use rectangles (which can be resized into squares), ellipses (which can be resized into circles) or rounded rectangles. You could also demonstrate how to make shapes using the polygon tool.

● Colour can be added to the shapes by clicking the Fill tool (a paint pot falling over), selecting a colour from the palette at the bottom of the screen, and then clicking inside the shape.

● Save children's patterns and view them on the whiteboard. Ask the rest of the class to identify each pattern and ask questions, for example: *If you continue the pattern, which shape would come next? What is the second shape? Which shape comes after the circle?*

You Can... **Use an interactive whiteboard to improve children's performance in PE**

PE lessons encourage active participation, and also encompass other elements such as performance, strategy, skills practice and the process of review and evaluation. The use of an interactive whiteboard is particularly useful for the evaluation of children's performance in PE. You can use digital photography and video or film clips for this purpose. However, ICT can also be used for a range of related activities, for example, knowledge and understanding of fitness and health.

Thinking points

● Always obtain permission from parents prior to filming or photographing children.

● When using the whiteboard for PE, allot small amounts of time for this during the day. This will ensure that time allocated for practical work is not consumed. Ideally, these time slots should be just before a break, or just after the children have settled down following quiet reading.

● Use photographs, and digital video taken during PE lessons to inform your planning and assessment. This type of evidence can be invaluable as a mental and visual reminder when you are writing reports.

● Use photographs or video clips to illustrate your teaching points. Decide upon your focus in advance, for example, style, balance, teamwork or fluency of movement.

● Think about how you will encourage the children to evaluate their work. A balance shown on a slide, for example, could be annotated with a thick whiteboard pen to show the correct position.

● Subject to copyright, explore the use of video clips from dance companies depicting dances from different times, places and cultures.

Tips, ideas and activities

● During a lesson on different types of balances, use a digital camera to take pictures of each balance. Take pictures of good single and paired balances, as well as balances which could be improved. Display these on the whiteboard and ask children to evaluate them. Ask open-ended questions to encourage children to extend their answers. The Primary National Strategy's *Learning and Teaching Using ICT* (2004) includes specific activities for reviewing children's performance in PE using the interactive whiteboard. These include lesson plans, pupil activities and video clips.

● Take five digital photographs of different gymnastic movements. Display these on a flipchart, in a random order. Ask the children to perform the movements in the pictures, one after the other. When they have finished, ask a child to arrange the images in a different order. Ask the class to perform the new routine on the board. Which routine was better? Why?

● Use ICT for a range of activities related to PE, for example, athletics, orienteering, and knowledge and understanding of fitness and health. Use heart monitors to measure heart beats during a race, or navigate around a course using a Roamer. Respond to the evidence provided by these activities in the classroom, using the whiteboard.

You Can... Use an interactive whiteboard to create simple musical compositions

Music composition programs are ideally suited for the interactive whiteboard. Such programs are often similar to computer games in which musical notation or icons are dragged and dropped into a frame on the screen. Some packages, such as Compose World Junior *(ESP software), are loaded with hundreds of musical phrases that, when used together, can create a range of songs. On an interactive whiteboard, with the speakers plugged in, they look and sound good and are fun to use.*

Thinking points

● Ensure that the composition program fits the objectives you are covering. There are several composition programs available that have excellent production values, but do not necessarily have appropriate applications in the classroom.

● Many programs do not allow the user to save their work. If this is the case, ask children to note down or print out their final musical arrangements so they can reproduce them. Alternatively, screen shots can be taken and displayed on the whiteboard for review.

● Consider how the children will listen to their music whilst composing it – headphones are an essential requirement. Finished pieces can also be displayed on the interactive whiteboard for the whole class to see and hear.

● SMART Board and Promethean ACTIVboard software both contain their own sound recorder, which can be used to record sounds generated in the classroom.

● The image library in your whiteboard may provide useful software for the creation of musical compositions.

Tips, ideas and activities

● There are many very useful resources available in the 'music room' at www.bbc.co.uk/schools/communities/onionstreet. This site provides a range of musical themes, the potential to download a mixer, and links to resources from around the world, to enable children to create their own music.

● Plan a project linking ICT to music. The children, in groups, can compose a piece of music using composition software (or actual instruments). They can then prepare a PowerPoint presentation, with images that match the mood of the piece. This can be presented to, and reviewed by, the whole class using the whiteboard. The benefit of using composition software is that the pieces can be organised and reorganised as required.

● Create a set of musical cards on the whiteboard. Prepare some Clip Art images of musical instruments with their associated sounds. Ask the children to identify each instrument's sound, and describe its timbre (or quality).

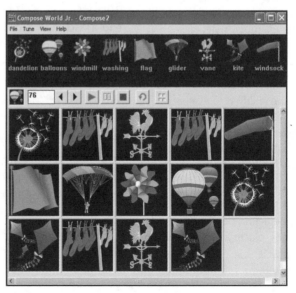

From *Compose World Junior,* ESP software

You Can... **Use an interactive whiteboard to investigate colour and texture**

There are many paint packages available for ICT. Children enjoy using these packages and they help to develop their artistic understanding. Demonstrating the use of paint packages on the whiteboard not only shows how these programs can be used, but also illustrates to children how creative and inspiring digital art can be. If you do not have any paint software, use the palette available on Microsoft Word to investigate colour. For example, you can create different coloured squares and arrange them next to each other in different combinations as a basis for discussion about colour.

Thinking points

● Simple paint packages offer a lot of different functions and have tremendous potential for painting and drawing. Keep things simple to start with. Introducing and following just two techniques can produce some really striking work.

● Some degree of colour blindness is not uncommon. Be aware that one or two children may not be able to easily distinguish between all shades. Consider changing backgrounds (see below) to make a painting or image accessible to all.

● The whiteboard cannot substitute for the real experience of creating collages and paintings. Use the whiteboard to introduce children to different techniques and processes and to review children's work at the end of a lesson.

● Explore the different tools available in the paint package or on the whiteboard software: for example, use the Spray tool to demonstrate colour and light, or the Fill tool to create visual effects.

Tips, ideas and activities

● Scan in children's painted pictures and display them on the whiteboard. Ask the rest of the class what colours and colour mixes have been used to create the paintings. Then ask the artists themselves.

● Some paint packages allow colour mixing. Ask children to predict, for example, what happens when blue and yellow are mixed.

● Display a small part of a painting and ask children to describe the colours they can see.

● Ask children what colours or shades they would use to paint a sky. Display just the sky from a well-known painting (for example, Van Gogh's *A Cornfield with Cypresses*). Examine it closely, to show children the many different colours that have been used.

● Create a firework picture for Bonfire Night using an art package such as Paint. Create a black background by selecting the Fill icon. Talk with the children about which colours will show up best and use various tools, such as the Airbrush, to create firework effects. Display children's pictures on the whiteboard to discuss the effects and the colours used. Add the children's names in text boxes to make a whole-class 'gallery'.

You Can... **Use an interactive whiteboard to show and compare places of worship**

It has always been a challenge to get hold of appropriate religious artefacts and pictures for whole-class work. With a whiteboard and the Internet, these resources can be accessed easily and cheaply, and can be enlarged so that they are accessible to all. Many children will have little or no experience of religious artefacts or buildings, so resources such as these are very useful. Always check copyright when downloading, scanning or in any way manipulating pictures.

Thinking points

● Collect suitable pictures of religious buildings. If you live near different places of worship, ask for permission to photograph them. Learning will be reinforced by the proximity of these buildings to where the children live. If it is not possible to take photos, then search the Internet for suitable pictures or use Clip Art images.

● Remember to save your photographs. They can then be accessed at any time and for different purposes.

● Look out for video resources which not only show the outside of religious buildings but also feature a guided tour of the inside, and explain the significance of artefacts.

● There is no substitute for an actual visit to a local place of worship. Schools are made very welcome and it is a memorable experience for the children. Use the whiteboard to introduce the idea of the visit, and to review children's experiences of it.

Tips, ideas and activities

● Use the images of religious buildings that you have collected and saved to create a PowerPoint presentation. Click Insert and find the picture icon. Search for your saved picture and click Insert again. The picture will appear in the slide. Give the picture a title.

● Add a title slide detailing the objective of the lesson. Add slides before and after each of the picture slides and use these to ask key questions. When you play the presentation to the children, discuss each slide in turn. Return to the title slide at the end of the lesson to review what the children have learned.

● Alternatively, encourage groups of children to put together the presentation. Ask them to draw out similarities and differences between the different religious buildings and to write these on the board, or to annotate the pictures using the Pen or Highlighter tools.

● Encourage the children to prepare a 'script' for their presentation, and to decide who will deliver it. Allow them time to rehearse the presentation and to practise using the whiteboard tools.

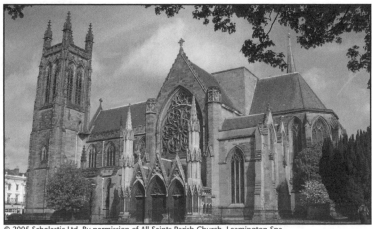

© 2005 Scholastic Ltd. By permission of All Saints Parish Church, Leamington Spa.

Whiteboard diary

Teacher's name: _____

Date	Subject/ Objective	How was the whiteboard used?	Evaluation

Whiteboard resources library

Teacher's name: _____

Name of resource and file location	Description of resource	How resource was used	Date resource was used

Lesson planning using the whiteboard

Title of lesson

Objectives
- Be clear about what you want the children to learn.

Prior learning
- Review what children already know, or need to be reminded of before the lesson.

Vocabulary
- Think about the key words children need to recall during the lesson. Should these be displayed on the whiteboard?

How will the whiteboard be used?
- Decide whether to use the whiteboard for the starter, the main teaching activity or the plenary session.

Starter activity
- Decide upon the purpose of the starter.
- Consider whether you will need to refer back to any prior learning or saved files from earlier whiteboard lessons.
- If preparing resources for the whiteboard, decide how long each will take to work through, given the time available for a starter activity.
- Keep a record of any screens used.
- Check copyright restrictions before using images from websites.

Main activity
- Think about the sequence of what you will do and what you want the children to do.
- Prepare the learning resources for the whiteboard before the lesson, including displaying the lesson objectives and using illustrations wherever possible.
- Keep the teaching and learning activities concise, using no more than three or four screens.
- Write down any questions you may need to ask the children.
- Plan what the children will do for their group or independent learning activities.

Plenary session
- Ask the children what they have found out.
- Prepare questions to ask the children.
- Decide whether you will ask children to present any of their learning on the whiteboard. If so, allow additional time for them to prepare their materials.
- Think about whether you will need to refer back to any whiteboard resources presented earlier in the lesson.
- Finally, refer back to the learning objectives presented at the start of the lesson to consolidate children's learning.

After the lesson
- Write down the links to schemes of work as well as to the National Curriculum.
- Make a note of any books or websites you may have used.
- Make a quick note of anything you would do differently.
- Save the lesson plan in both a paper and electronic file so that you can find it easily next time.
- You may find it helpful to save whiteboard screens that have been annotated with children's ideas, so that you can adjust your original lesson if you wish to use it again.

Additional Resources

Advice

- Becta, which is responsible to the DfES for ICT in education, provides advice on the use of whiteboards at **www.ictadvice.org.uk** To access the information you require simply input 'whiteboards' into the search facility on the site.

- Becta also offers advice and guidance for schools thinking of purchasing interactive whiteboards under the 'Interactive whiteboards project'. This section of the site summarises the equipment that is available under the scheme. **www.becta.org.uk/leaders/leaders.cfm?section-3_1&id=3170**

Classroom resources

- The National Whiteboard Network at **www.nwnet.org.uk** provides resources for whiteboard use across the curriculum and advice on accessing whiteboard software. Teachers are also encouraged to add their own resources to the site.

- Whiteboard manufacturers Promethean and SMART Board both provide resources for teaching and learning and case studies of whiteboard use.
Weblinks: **www.prometheanworld.com/uk/**
www.smartboard.co.uk/

- There are many free resources available for use with the whiteboard at **www.bbc.co.uk/schools** and **www.standards.dfes.gov.uk/primary/mathematics** The Standards Site includes a range of free mathematical tools that may be downloaded for use with the whiteboard within the Interactive teaching programs (ITPs).

- EDpaX Ltd have designed a step-by-step program of interactive whiteboard lessons aligned directly to the National Curriculum. Visit **www.edpax.com** for further information

- The Ready Resources series (Scholastic) is a multimedia package which comprises a CD-ROM full of classroom material, and a comprehensive book of teacher's notes. The images, sound, video and text are all specially chosen to match the curriculum and the QCA Schemes of Work. **www.scholastic.co.uk/readyresources**

- Penpals for Handwriting CD-ROM (Cambridge Hitachi), is a resource for teaching handwriting designed for use with an interactive whiteboard. Included are teacher's notes and homework sheets for each unit. Available at **www.cambridge.org**

Additional Resources

● Available from TTS Group Ltd, the QX5 Computer Microscope includes presentation software for slideshows and videos of the children's work on the whiteboard. There is also a companion booklet available separately.
Weblink: **www.tts-group.co.uk**

● The Olympus C-770 is a 3.9 megapixel digital camera which can be used with a whiteboard. It incorporates a 1.8" LCD screen and a 10× optical zoom. See **www.olympus.co.uk**

● Nikon make a 7 megapixel digital camera which will take video with audio. The Coolpix 7900 has a long battery life which can take 220 images, and includes a 2" LCD screen. Visit **www.nikon.co.uk** for further details.

Videos
● To see many and varied examples on video of whiteboards being used across the primary curriculum look out for the Primary National Strategy: *Learning and Teaching Using ICT* resource. This resource consists of a pack of CD-ROMs, for each year including the Foundation Stage and supports the use of ICT and whiteboards across all subjects. The pack was available free to schools in 2004. Contact the DfES Publications Centre at dfes@prolog.uk.com; tel 0845 60 222 60.

Research
● For details of research on interactive whiteboards and case studies of whiteboard practice go to **client.cant.ac.uk/ research/papers**